D1598899

SiNEW

10 YEARS OF POETRY IN THE BREW

2011 - 2021

APRIL GLOAMING

Publisher's Cataloguing-in-Publication Data

Sinew: 10 years of poetry in the brew, 2011-2021 / written by multiple
authors / edited by Jo Collins, Christine Hall, Matthew Johnstone, and
Henry L. Jones / proofread by Lance Umenhofer
  ISBN: 978-1-953932-06-8

1. Poetry Anthologies: General I. Title

EDITED BY:

Jo Collins
Christine Hall
Matthew Johnstone
Henry L. Jones

PROOFREAD BY:

Lance Umenhofer

Contents

7

CONTENTS

Spirit

FOREWORD
Christine Hall

Nashville in the 90s smelled like a city coming awake. Known as a musical hub and the setting for pivotal civil rights campaigns, Nashville invited creative and progressive minds to converge. The arts flourished, while the small town feel lingered, manifesting in conviviality between passersby on the street and collaborations aplenty.

In this environment ripe for renaissance, poetry hit a heyday. Poetry open mics popped up in a variety of places. As a teen, I visited a few, lurking in the back and taking notes, reveling in this atmosphere where the muse's presence made itself evident.

Amidst the many changes that come with rapid growth, 2011 saw Nashville poets without a dedicated open mic. Securing a new location at Portland Brew East, the founders of Poetry in the Brew welcomed an inclusive group of poets, spoken word artists, and storytellers. The community gathered in the loft of this coffeeshop on the second Saturday of each month, connecting through trials and triumphs, sharing poetry. Even as original members moved on, the community continued expanding, heralding returning readers and newcomers alike.

Poets formed familial bonds—including two marriage proposals that happened at the Brew—and embarked on successful projects, some attracting international recognition. At the onset of the pandemic in 2020, Poetry in the Brew transitioned to weekly online open mics. This gave ease of accessibility to visitors from all over the world, not just those passing through Nashville. Emerging and established voices join in vulnerable and fervent expressions, dubbing it poetry church.

On the occasion of our 10th anniversary in 2021, we celebrate with this anthology. Through the creative exchange in which we participate, we deepen our views, our engagement with one another, and our experiences of poetry.

This sinew that binds and supports us is what we have to show for making poetry of all that comes and embracing each other along the way.

FLESH

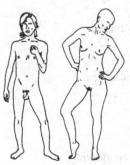

SEASONS + US
Ali El-Chaer

I.
I feel like mint left in the sun,
And my repetition is ancient.
We teach the children to dry their herbs,
And how to save it for later.
Maybe to share over food.
Maybe to put in tea.
The humidity reminds me of what I was.

II.
Dried,
I can be crushed by hand.
I'm just a summertime herb to you.

III.
Why did you even plant me?
Don't you know how quickly I spread?
I am *invasive*,
But you brought me here willingly.

IV.
You had plenty of time to learn,
how to care for me.

V.
So why are you surprised,
When my resistance is to keep growing,
Long after you've dried my parts on the porch,
And salted the earth.

IT SEEMS I WANT YOU ONLY WITH MY GUT
Allison Boyd Justus

cathedrals groan assent
                    to i know not what

pears rotted in the kitchen while i loved you

Monologue to an Oatmeal Moon
Christian J. Collier

Let me sing to you of what happened
right before you stumbled upon your throne.
The wind dipped its fingers into the pigeon gray back of the lake & stirred
a spell I could not look away from.

The beauty broke me from
the unwonder of the current time that killed my friend,   but as I stared on in reverenc
one mosquito gruffly taxied through
the evening's peach crescendo   & left with a piece of me & my blood in its throat.

That slight beast did   the most male & American of acts, thieved
what belonged to me without consent.
Now, a sliver of my legacy has had to erect
a tent in the belly of a new earth   amid a torrent of acids & apparitions.

That quick kiss caused
the instruments of the near-night
to unfurl me,   sent a stream of
what has gone missing sweeping by –

its scent,   stroking the cavern of my nostrils.
I wondered, as the drum roll from its wings grew more mute
each second it escaped beyond me,
if this was what intimacy meant now

in the era of the longed-for touch.
Interveniente,
one virus clamoring to replace the maraud of another & either way,
the body belongs not wholly to itself,

the body becomes taken treasure,   a means to sate something else's need to be fed.
but this is nothing new.
Consumption is always what becomes of the body
if it exists in the world long enough.

The body is always in season to be mashed by the teeth of one being or another
that is tired of dining only on dark air.
Dear moon,
do you know how filled with want I'd been

16

before that black bug's tiny sting came?
How strongly
I had been thirsting   for something breathing to taste me?
When his small mouth heard me & wallowed in my sweet & salt,

I did not once think to raise my hands & clap the life out of him.   Instead,
I combed the bridge of my palm over the shaded place he drank from
attempting to close the short doors he left stranded open   when
he pulled his slender lips away from me.

SKIN
Donna Krupkin Whitney

The scab on my arm is the same shape
As the crescent of orange peel in my negroni.
Beneath the brown crust
Fibroblasts creep across filaments of fibrin
And enthusiastic epithelial cells link hands to make skin.
The color and markings of my skin
Tell me more about myself than I ever asked to know.
But now I know.

This morning a hummingbird found me on my deck,
And came almost close enough to kiss.
His lavish emerald greeting was a message, I think,
From the bluebird and the roadrunner
Who were my gentle father's friends.
For real, those two birds and Daddy were friends.
His last words to Mother were "I love you."
The last thing he said to me was, "Don't take shit from anyone."

Most mornings I'm glad to see the sun
But some days dreams surround me like a cloud
And I have to sleep off the drug we called marriage.
Under my quilt
The warm fragments of me reach for one another
And I am a shiny planet
A coalescence of primordial atoms hungry for each other's company
And in my dreams, I am comfortable in my own skin.

VISCOSITY
Andrew P. Dillon

Love keeps things
lubricated. Fingers,
lips, knees, even,
distribute the grease.
All moving parts
require regular
exchanges of fluid.
Try to start
an engine without
oil on the pistons.
Count how many
strokes before
everything seizes up.

RABBIT SKIN
Phynne~Belle (Tricia De Jesus-Gutierrez)

I am terrified by the light
I see burned upon your ribs
I used to wear this mantle when
I too was a concoction of impressionable

onion paper doll on my freshly
laid mother soil

I clung fast to puncturing edges
I was good deeds and lovely features

-by-association when encircled in
the thick-set covetous arms

You are blameless and this makes
you believe that it is only goodness

heaped laurel leaves and fragrant posies
upon your crown, you are cosseted
and are spoon fed an evil who cannot be
so simple still you are told this as truth

You have no reason to turn it over in the sunlight
You have no purpose for asking why

WOLVES LICK THEIR WOUNDS
Noel Marie

Eroded guts
Smell smoke
Where's the fire love?
Unlaced feelings.
Dust bunnies dance.
Flesh, flesh all a mess!
Your skin is salty truth.
Ghosts. They don't
Hide. I see them too.
Naked. Sucking shame
Pop. They know.
Destruct. Blood in the sink.
The sun shines down
On my breasts.
Howling wolves.
I begin to lick my knees.
Taste like home.

Living Templo
Edith Tapia "Blackbird"

Caminando por la calle,
feminidad, masculinidad, and all.
Hips sway right, left, right, left, right, left.

I feel like I should every day, you know,
como un templo viviente, a living temple,
it walks, breathes, habla, envejece and all,
a piece of art,
único como podrás ver.

There's no serial number on me, son,
there's no replacement of me under warranty,
nadie como yo allá afuera en tierra brava,
not even an evil twin, doppelganger, or clone could do the trick.
Nada de eso ¿comprendes?
Did you really get it?

I don't believe you did, no te creo.
So let me tell you something real quick,
escucha atentamente,
this king/queen/queer belongs to consent.

Fácil de entender: sí, es sí. No, es no.
You feel me?

Then, what are you thinking, Mr. Somebody?
¿Qué me miras?
Yes, look at this body as a miracle of life,
just like your own,
sí, admira la belleza en éste cuerpo si quieres,
there's no problem for me,
but hey! Don't look at me so thirsty, dude.
No me mires como un canival a punto de atacar.

Wait! What the fuck is your hand doing
trespassing my sacred bubble?
¿Qué hacen tus intenciones yendo hacia mi intimidad?
one foot, one inch, un centímetro, un soplido...
just about to land on forbidden ground,
ignorando mi vestido,
ignoring the warning signs,
mi dignidad,
the common sense,
my right to stay peaceful
mientras disfruto de mi templo tranquilamente.

I told you before,
this body is a living temple,
engineering cell machine
forged by energy with infinite names,
una maravilla caminante
que otras maravillas pueden presenciar,
hammered by years and battles yet to end.

See my scars, these wounds?
Sí, estas marcas sobre mi cuerpo y alma ¿las ves?
proof of quality over quantity, honey,
valiente ser que despierta cada día rodeada de gente como tú.

Now listen,
I won't convince you to treat your body with respect,
but I will make you treat mine like you should,
no rogaré porque te ames a tí mismo
pero cuidado con querer romperme ¿comprendes?

Because I used to be an always yes, sir, yes, ma'am.
I used to be a war zone.
Mi cuerpo era tierra de todos menos mío,
where everyone could dig in my soul,
use their weapons on my skin,
donde podían romper, quebrar, excavar, extraer,
amasar, robar, irse y jamás volver, dejándome desolada.
They used to take whatever was left
since my voice was under a white flag all the time.

Always yes, yes, yes,
sí para todos menos para mí misma.
Take a piece of me, yes!
toca aquí y allá cuando te plazca, sí,
pour your venom through my lips, yes!
seal my ears with bitch, useless, puta, pendeja, yes!
abusame cuando lo desees, sí,
always yes, yes, yes!
but not anymore, my dear,
¡ya no más!

I'm on my way to reclaim my rights, my voice,
en una batalla conmigo misma y ellos
para recuperar mi voz.
About to put a fire mark of consent on your forehead,
a ver si así lo olvidas.

Unfortunately, if you look around,
harassment, el maldito acoso,
still has a place in this society,
in my survival instincts,
tiene un lugar en mi puño,
my pepper spray,
mi navaja de bolsillo,
my taser,
la fuerza de quien me acompaña.

But why? ¿Por qué el acoso aún existe?
harassment shouldn't be a commander
for anybody to break the fence
and lick someone else's roots,
nadie debería corromper mis raíces y las tuyas,
impulsados por sus bajos intintos,
and take PTSD as a souvenir.
¡No señor, no!

So let me tell you one last time,
a ver si por fin te queda claro:
¿Ves éste cuerpo? sí, este cuerpo es un templo viviente.
This king/queen/queer belongs to consent.
Cuando digo sí es sí, cuando digo no es no.

I have the choice to howl, calling my pack, see?
and you have the choice
to take your invader privilege ass out of my playground,
de largarte de mi templo y arrastrarte en tu propia miseria allá solo.

You feel me now? I hope so…

VALENTINE FOR A MONK
Jon Wesick

He shaved his head
and wore a robe made from a burial shroud.
She had gray eyes, blonde hair, and a body
her mother taught her never to be ashamed of.

She baked him brownies
and gave him a heart-shaped card
listing what she loved about him.
"You're calm, kind, and at home
in the here and now."

To escape this world, he must forgo
what's most worthy in this world
so he tried not to see her. That failed
when he glimpsed her toned arm
imagining it around his shoulder.
Next, he considered her a collection of parts –
skin, muscle, bone, fat, bile,
snot, urine, and feces. That failed
when the music of her voice
sang an aria of affection.
So, he pictured the inevitable,
her body as a corpse, swollen and putrid.

She rested a hand on his forearm,
wishing her love into a pillow
to cushion his dreams
and her body a blanket
to protect him.

The Buddha had said a monk's robe
should be his only armor but her finger
so gentle yet so strong
stuck in a tear through its sleeve.

Did I Ever Tell You That Your Mouth Is Like
Michelle Awad

fireflies, freshly bloomed cotton waving in the wind,
around 60 degrees, a hand on my belly; that is to say,
your mouth is like a sign of life, a conception, a well full
of blue ink. Like a matchstick between the teeth to stop my
eyes watering. Like the silken head of a baby bird under
my first two fingertips. Like when I warm my hands in your
shirtsleeves. Like a flowing sieve.
I press myself against your lips, cold, like steel wrapped
in suede; that is to say, my body is like a shotgun with your
mouth around it, something you stare down the barrel of daily,
and your lips, a soft pillow, your tongue a muzzle, you search
for the trigger with your hips, and your mouth, your
delicate mouth, all gauze and cold compress,
and petroleum jelly,
a motive that can't break through
my teeth.

HANDS
Landrew Sevel

I. *To be read with one hand gently on your throat*

the line deep and pulling
to surface is defiance, broken allegiance
with the only through and then still here
maybe it will rain as if rain were a choice
to be two places at once, we
remember that even without it
purged and then nourishment for some
very beauty temporary, the cloud will
always be changed, lighter in its path

digging into the ground, softened
for something to jump out, relic
in hand, in downpour, in drowning
they say the world, our bodies change
sizes, silently howl, not knowing
the transition from cloud to gone,
to absence measured in green

weeping and rage share waters
somewhere far away, invisible
cliffs of skyward falls, another mouth
pours, screams itself inside out
space changing how the light moves
through, now stealing nothing until
it rains, crossing itself again

II. *To be read with both hands cradling your lower ribs*

unsettled ache from gripping
the ground seeks its own movement
but instead just tears, holding
to both hopes of timelessness, odd warmth,
and desperation to be out, beyond,
to once again digestible death
tallied to bear the possibility of beauty,
being weightless almost, in a lingering flash
of that which is all we are, were, really
gone before the spark faced the only
demise there ever was,
desire becoming a source of misdoubt,
singed, pulling in to wall rather than ripple,
mirror of skin and skin of essence
in condensation,
in ever expansion, shining
to be the constellation of your desires, all
plural as the formation itself,
held together the space between
finger and ground by no thing
but the waiting from the stars

Human Skin Tag
Jo Collins

god gave me the exact right amount of skin
To cover my bones
But I just had to make more

I wanted it 3 inches deep
A suit of armor
An electric fence to keep the dogs out
Oh, how they growled
And taunted me with quiet yelps
That sounded like newborn babies crying

My sinking womb floated to the surface
Lurched and pulsed like a starfish
Regrowing its missing limb

A minor infraction
Of my unspoken oath
To fit neatly in a drawer
No trouble at all
Just a pile of skin, folded like a sweater

ME/AT
Ananda Lima

— *"Eu já vivo enjoado" introduction* —

In the red light of late
afternoon I stand clean
and naked in the
                              post
shower fog with
 a bleary reflection
 of this body of mine
  of yours and I want to
                              call
the conference of my face
 summon us from
                              this
body of mine of
 yours but I don't
                              know
how to sift through
 the indices of pronouns
in our languages
                              I
  want you to
  confess twisting
  the proteins of
                              your
  mouths masked
in the muscles in
 my cheeks as
                              I
 wipe wet my
hands wrinkled
 with condensation
                              and

31

stare at this face of
yours of mine asking
                    what
  have you done
to us what have we
  done to you can
                    I
claim you as you
  did one another
                    my
voice echoes and I get
closer to the cleared
  path fogging again
cold silver surface still
                    open
my mouth and exhale as
                    we
hide in this meat of me
  this soft present
                    skin

after Nathaniel Mackey
and Mestre Pastinha

FEELING BODY LISTENING
Dane Ince

My perfect wonder amazes me with more questions
I pick them like ripe peaches
I eat them juicy and raw
Perfectly sweetly
Juice drops drips everywhere bloody
Summer sunburn the empty aching
Sizzle of bare feet on sidewalk
Beer bottle broken glass
Asphalt
Lone Star or Schlitz
Hopping to hop
Like a lion's bloody muzzle
A riot
Another dreary visit to the scene of the crime
Wonder about the edges of the hole of you
Do you slice your fingers on it still?
When you run pinkies and thumbs along its edge
To assure
Still there?
Sharpest cutting dull beware
Or has it been long enough
That the sharp edge rolls over
Like a dull kitchen knife?
Resting head on chest
Listening to heartbeat
Listening to love
For an embarrassingly long time
As long as it takes to smell every smell of grass
In the afternoon summer dream of a nap

SILENCE DREAMS
Tricia Schwaab

Last night I dreamed
of cancer
come into my throat,
limiting my speech
without surprise.

My massage therapist,
he had told me once
if you watch what
you say too long,
if you hold your truths
too tight,
your voice will disappear.
He told me this
a warning perhaps too late.

I hear my voice cracking,
feel the muscles
in my neck tightening,
straining to tell truths
few want to hear.

And now I dream of cancer,
my throat becoming
unable to speak
and I wonder if it's
already too late.

PRESENT/ABSENT
Hil Hoover

The baby goth in my rearview window
Wanted to believe that
There was something special
About being elusive
That it was possible to pretend
Unreliability was a virtue
Would make one missed and treasured

That it could be a cameo
Even if you weren't famous
And not simply being a background extra
A forgettable face in every crowd
That the right words at the right time
Could be enough
Even if that time was once a year

When the job went from full to part time
And the relationships dissolved into nothing
When the guild found new officers and no one
Remembered the quirky username on the favorite forum
When the plots in every writing group
Moved forward too quickly to follow
And the library books followed the milk to expiration

And still, I say,
I want to be invited to every event
Sit down at the buffet table of the internet
And lick my lips over a feast I can never devour
Watch the dates and times go by like
So many road signs
As the accelerator sticks in my car again
Headlong toward certain death.

And when I manage, finally, one small moment of connection
It's everything (great and fearful)
Distracting from my own face on the video -
Always the most grotesque thing in the room to my own eyes -
With the softness and weight of a plush toy
Distracting from my fear over the sound of my voice -
What are they hearing now? -
With laughter over the near-cartoon image of
Someone eating their snacks vigorously
Or the sheer cuteness of someone else's smile
The curly mop of a peering child
Or the swish of a cat's tail at the edge of a screen.

I want to be the globetrotting hero
And indeed in many ways I have become spoiled
Have been blessed with virtual visitors
From countries I myself will never visit
Have laughed at the antics of Canada or England
Sobbed over Ireland, sang with the heart of Malaysia,
Swooned over Australia, snapped along with India,
Closed my eyes and smiled to Scotland,
Eavesdropped Japan as if I remembered
Enough of the language to understand anything.

And yet, here I am,
Back home in the Boro,
Shifting constantly before the camera,
Wondering if anyone notices that face I am making
Or if it looks like I am only paying attention
If it is written across every feature that the pain is too much

36

Checking and double-checking the mute button
Because I don't want anyone to hear me
Heavy-breathing like a pervert on the line -
I remember this is not the event for perversion
Is not the space for shockingly sexual -
Shifting shoulders and hips and knees and legs
Stretching my back and biting my lip on the harsh groan

And wanting to be something other than elusive
Something other than illness and exhaustion
Something ethereal as the silken words of my peers
Poetic as this person's energy, that person's wit,
This one's dancing and stained lips,
The tremor of one reader and the cocky grin of another
Or the tone of voice that makes me wish it
Were not creepy to say "could you make me a voice message
For putting me to sleep?"

Am I here? Was I here?

I heard your voices, saw your faces,
Turned off the camera at some point so that I could
Do the stretches that make these broken pieces
Almost bearable,
Hid the tears that may have been about a turn of phrase
Or a creak of bone against bone
Kept my earbuds on until the last moments of farewell
Breathed everything in
Came away no less elusive, no more likely to
Step into the next event, the next, the next
A million missed opportunities
But quietly - all the same -
Grateful.

BORN
Nina Adel

She keeps waking up
with the same revelation,
like it's new,
every morning:
tagged. at birth. Father
held this latest baby in
its blanket, traced
radiating circles
alternating beige and blue
and red
onto its forehead with
his pointer finger.
the finger hairy at
the knuckles bending only
slightly. its tiny
Mediterranean curls.
adorable.
adored by women. and his wife.
the whole
of possibility still ahead,
but this baby,
small and last in line,
all mapped out now
in beige and blue
and red.
circles.

Kissing on the other hand, leaves the teeth well out of it, and they, at other times, do all the hard work. The tongue dips in and out occasionally to give assistance.

Mouths, where would we be without them?
Me, whenever I don't quite know what to do with my tongue, I place it firmly in my cheek.

MADONNA & CHILD
Des Mannay

"Shall we play dogs?"
she says. Imagination
kissed by childhood...

All games are real -
join in,
lost in time.

Entwined with her mother.
soul mate -
not cell mate.

Asks direct questions.
I give honest answers -
dance around moral handbags.

Hung up pre-hangover.
Close again - breath on skin.
We drunkenly sing.

Massage pain away.
Leave part of me.
Reclaim it one day

NOTE TO SELF
Andi Talbot

Before you start
lock the door
shut the blinds
draw the curtains
and remember where everything is
as it is
as it was
as it must be when we're done

Take photos of the order of clothes
to make sure all is as it should be
be certain to note
which hanger
and which way it's hung
can't be too careful
though
it's
not like she'd notice

See what's on offer tonight
curse her for taking my favourite shade
find my solitary brush
and resign myself to making the best of
what has been left behind

Another vital rule;

Always upstairs
never downstairs
and no matter what
no matter how cocky you get
NEVER
ON the stairs

That would be one way to let her know
Wouldn't it?
before she's ready
and before I'm ready
the key turns
the door opens
her jaw opens
and I'm just lying there
looking absolutely STUNNING
but in need of severe medical attention

But above all else
before we begin
make sure wipes and remover
are available
can't risk her catching me
with my eyes closed
and her pants down.

Ninth Life
Christine Hall

In your clown suit, with the broken handle and scraped knuckle
you loom in the doorway
in rage against the machinations of humanity
disguised as your fight to consume
to be consummate in this consumption
and to be consumed
the top notes of gasoline and coffee mingle in the street
similarity breeds familiarity
If you're going to show me the same shit you've shown me
a million times, show me this shit
a fool's grin, a leer
a nonsensical whim

I live at the brim
entertain guests with sips, draughts, synthesis
pulled from a wide selection of ingredients and well mixed
to muddle specific influence
this one's trailer trash is this same one's
treasured childhood past
see my foolish grin and raise me one that's menacing
teeth are the foundations of life
we cleaned our trailers up real nice
our folks fled theirs for a false reality
Daddy smoked crack, my mama was bulimic
I'm a bleeder
I pop zits, slash my wrists, have heavy periods
Bloodletting is a fine cure for no problems
for instance the shadow of melanin above my lips
age spots, the lives our livers have lived
To the fullest
it's only through self esteem this low that
we come to accept the opposite, we are infinitesimal
and the infinite

We are neoraunch carnival
We boldly go into the common grounds
to track down our individual peace
strip our kidskin pyjamas
shed foolhardy control mechanisms generated before we knew enough
to be embarrassed of our own tastes
our gut instinct based on bacterial profiling
We wield our meddling with the gall to call it good intentions, hell in heels
skips along gold bricks on the way to Grandma's
and over the Styx
red hands carry the basket
red hands hold the purse strings
pull the strings on Mama's red apron
Mama's in bed with the butcher man
mining teeth, minding the wolf she feeds
tying the pieces of her heart with string, packages of meat
meant for giving

He drinks to dull himself to the jagged edges of his own broken heart
I make certain my death is flavored with numbness and you
carney geek, jester, king of bullshit, eponymous
king of Hades, I view you as a little more fucked up
than me, which means I'm more fucked up than I'm willing to see.

46

OPIOIDS
Cathy Carson

24 hours since my last opioid
I can feel it starting soon
So, I gather what I need
Base camp is the spare room
I have a heat pack for the shivers
A cold pack for the sweats
And a basin for the vomiting
That hasn't started yet.

See I've done this so many times
I know all the tricks
Like, if you put your wrists in ice
It stops you feeling sick
The tapping has already started
Next the ticking, then the rock
Then the shivers then the nausea
Then the watching of the clock.

48 hours since my last opioid
Squatting on the loo
With a basin on my knee
Because what else can I do?
My hair is damp and matted
My hands just won't stop shaking
If death came to get me now
There would be nothing for the taking.

And my scalp is so damn itchy
Scratching doesn't help
Christ I would love a tramadol
But there is none on the bathroom shelf
The medication numbs the pain
That fogginess is kinda nice
But it numbs the person I fought to become
It numbs everything in life.

72 hours since my last opioid
I am writhing on the bed
Boy scout knots in my belly
Lord the pressure in my head
There is an ocean of hollow sadness
It feels like I'm falling in
I am clinging to the edges
I don't think I can swim.

I know without the tablets
My body will be sore
But you see my daddy was a drinker
So, addiction scares me more
So even though a thousand bugs
Crawl just beneath my skin
On the other side of this
I won't be anything like him.

96 hours since my last opioid
A shaft of light across my room
I left the curtains that way
I knew that's what it would do.
That little bit of sunshine
Is my little ray of hope
I know I'm nearly there now
I feel like I can cope.

Yeah, I'm still a little ticky
My nerves are jagged raw
I am anxious and I'm tearful
And my gut begins to gnaw
I'm feeling kind of hungry
This is a good sign
I just need to eat and potter now
I just need to give it time.

Two weeks since my last opioid
So many ups and downs
Tantrums, tears and tetchiness
So many pointless rows.
It is usually two more weeks
Before thoughts clear and nerves calm
Long walks, hot baths, good food,
The love of a phenomenal man.
That long-suffering-husband
Who tells me I have been a bear
But I'll be back on form, living life full tilt
Until the next time fibro flares.

THE CIRCUS
Des Mannay

I can barely bring myself to go to the circus anymore,
to see the tightrope walkers.
To see those once subtle and well trained feet
now decaying, rotten and infested with maggots,
who urge each other on up through the legs
towards the heart of the beast.
Those wise old heads befuddled now -
making mistakes that you in your youthfulness can easily perceive.
And finally they fall, to perish on the ground - without a safety net.
But imagine if you will,
that you are forced to walk that tightrope.
With all those wise old heads in the audience
trying to guide those untrained obstinate feet of yours,
wishing you to make no mistakes.
And without a safety net...........

THE WAITING GAME MY BODY PLAYS
Franchesa Kirkpatrick

The waiting game my body plays.
Doctors say there is another test.
My body.
Here's the needle. Do your best.
My body.
My body is now a part of the waiting game.
No one knows what you have.
My body.
We will call you when we can fit you in.
My body.
The x rays, the MRIs, the CTs, the labs never end.
I do not think I got any rest last night.
My body.
The doctors did not call today.
My body.
The waiting game my body plays.

SHELTERED JOY
Henry L. Jones

There is a joy hidden from eyes
whether strangers, family or friends
who look and wonder what you're hiding

sometimes tears leak your joy
cascading from the eyes' edges
passing the salty nuggets of sleep

unremoved from the morning
damming some shuttled water
where fragments of your dreams

still clustered on the eyelashes
awaiting replayed memories
you face remains dry and stiff

you look for a cup of brew
to drink and welcome the day
longing to remember the joy

left in the draping pitch of night
vague images engulfed tightly
in a lover's arms making love

the dew still lingering on your thighs
now dry and brittle a forensic proof
someone touched and released you

from the dullness and loneliness
for a moment even if that joy
erupted from fantasy and thirst

people noticed the craving in your eyes
as you watched and smelled nearby
as warm fleshy mouth passed and smiled

wondering if the grin was an open
invitation to share a few moments
of passion taking and giving all

trying to replace the days of emptiness
filling and feeling the cold with warmth
until boiling simmers to a thick stew

condensing the broth left cooking
as you dared yourself to touch it
and allow a small leaking or taste

of yourself freeing the hunger
perhaps believing one spoonful
would drive you insane to keep eating

realizing the hunger still remains
no matter how much you stirred
and seasoned the pot with salt

gathering from the sweat trickling
dripping along the tenderness
falling off the bone onto the bed

where you lay trembling alone
reaching to the marrow of rivers
still cold inside but some warmth

fever so much life the flu
where your mind crazes like Alice
wondering if some tea will help

allow you to fall asleep soon
but no your covers are stale
with dried stains of lovers

so you clutch the nearest thing
a pillow or the mattress to cuddle
floating in the lake you poured

yourself on the sheets of passion
now wet and funky from yourself
a drizzling spring rain falling

you felt ashamed and filthy again
but needed that storm to come
so you hid the desire and look

hoping no one noticed your face
of sheltered joy a frail self locked
in the cage of your trapped desires.

I IIIMA GIN E
Kana Kavon

Yo u r laaa uggh rumb ling jus t b ehin d my earrr lob es
graaan it e che st prre sss   ed again st th e lime st on e col um n
of my spiii ne
broke n uuup fan ta sieees jing le   in m y pa lm
i wan t la aaaay y ou dow n in dis join ted liine s
an d stt tud y trrace maaap foll ow
th e con s tell at ions o f you r e-
ye s

MY BODY THE LILY OF THE VALLEY
Carolyn Connolly

after Calamus

My body the lily of the valley my
bell-scooped pale breasts dangling low
a chainmail necklace's droop between fingertips
as the years begin to pull me back down, slowly, back
into the earth my palms crusting over to the color
of burnt ochre— I am waiting for time to make
something beautiful of me— dry and soak
the pieces of my skin a ripe harvest in the fall
be ready to burn by the sage wand in winter.
I steal the petal off the cutting room floor I
tuck it safe into the pocket lining but I'd give
you the wheat stalks from my hair give
you the sunflower seeds from my socks
that fall from my pant legs like smoked rain and Jesus
wept so much blood that the earth yearned
for the taste of it sucking the salt right off
the tear yawning open the pit of the stomach until
a child's jar of fireflies breaks open
on the kitchen counter like a hardboiled egg.
My limbs a field of lavender moving
as one body one mind tilted to the side
of a sparrow's head bent over a sprig
of winterberry the other the mast of a ship battered
against a cliffside I promise you the tide
bears us in and spits us all out upon the
same sandy shoreline dirty and torn a fawn's
foot caught in barbwire— chin to chin calf to calf
thumb to thumb I cannot hold you without holding
myself a knot so intricate at the base
of the throat I open wider to let the wind
move about the furniture inside me even
as a chair hits the wall and splits in two.

I having gathered you here must leave you
in the home of lovers with only a gentle loneliness
to tell time by as the seasons out the window
turn the dawn's dew into an afternoon rain
the hurried breeze into a tornado alley storm—
but I am a bitter oil on the tongue I'd curl
the roof off if it meant I could hold you
even if the ceiling of the sky broke
even if the air held only sparks
even if we welcomed in the second flood
and could grab nothing else.

WILL YOU STILL WANT ME?
Navita Gunter

When the lights come on
And the make-up comes off
WILL YOU STILL WANT ME?!
When my weave turns into a shag
And my natural hair starts to recede
WILL YOU STILL WANT ME?!
When you discover that my feet are large STINK!
And I have hammer toes
WILL YOU STILL WANT ME?!
When the wrinkles start to show
And my steps grow slower
WILL YOU STILL WANT ME?!
When my HEALTH is less than perfect
And I grow tired much faster than I used to
WILL YOU STILL WANT ME?!
Something just HIT the door running
OHH OHH AND RUNNING! AND RUNNING!
And he told me that he had a broken ankle!
I guess I have my answer

EXILE ON MAIN STREET
Erin Gannon

My face was pock-marked
and I had the hairiest armpits.
It was pretty kinky
and sometimes
those boys looked
like they wanted to know.

The jeans I lived in
hadn't been washed
since 1987.

I was sleek, my crotch
all minx like an oil spill.
(Remember how Chuck Berry
once did a whole interview
with his face in between some chick's legs?)

My skin was too white for my black hair;
black widows crawled on my forearms, legs, eyebrows.
I could see every one of my muscles
but I probably couldn't have hurt anyone.

I had a Norplant
that fed my bloodstream as
I breathed, hormones that may yet give me
a heart attack if I keep smoking.
The Norplant was so I wouldn't get pregnant if someone
decided to fuck me
and find out about:
how my fingernails were
always short so they didn't hurt
very much when I scratched a man's back,
or how my come was Buckfast sweet
despite the level of my whiskey intake.

I cried, too, back then, but no one ever saw that.
By crying time, the spiders had overtaken their eyes,
(they'd be scared even of my eyelashes!)
and then it would all end, each and every one of them,
like they'd interviewed me
with their heads in between my legs.

UNTITLED #1
Craig Freeman

Have you ever caught the stare of a new found love
And wonder what do they see?

Scared they'll see the scars from your past.

You try to cover your flaws with your hands
But their fingertips
gliding across your goosebumps

Is an affirmation
that the only story they want to read is yours.

Is love blind?
I'm not sure.

But I know it reminds us
that sometimes
we need help seeing the beauty of our own story.

Muggy
Allison Boyd Justus

I don't want the truth to be known that I am but body,
living meat, scent of old deodorant,
sheathed by jewel-toned cardigan
I should have laundered last week after all,
to be safe, and the meeting's in eighteen minutes.

Hot damp scent, you demand
precisely angled air stream.
You require open
underarms: just so.
But not obvious.
Shoulders back, head high.
You request discretion.
I comply.

My colleague down the hall can exclaim over lunch
that she smells like a truck driver, provoking
bewildered laughter from the team, and if I could guffaw
about my own scent like that, should I?

O hot damp scent between the body and the arms, how we fear
discovery. We fear justified disgust, evidence for scorn.
We work to reign in any whiff which would proclaim
our own ineptitude, justify distrust.
We need the signatures.
We need consensus.
We need a good scrub with Dr. Bronner's peppermint soap.

O hot damp scent, I would dispel you with a hot long late-night shower,
but I will make do with a quick scrub,
paper towels and hand soap in the staff bathroom,
save deep clean for tomorrow morning to prevent your return.
Finish quick fix with emergency perfume: scent of lilac in the wrists.

O stale sweat-scent, you tell the truth we don't want out:
that the pace of this work is too much, and I was so fraught
last night I took a hot shower just to wind down,
so I was up late, so I slept late,
and I did what I could with my hair, and I am clean,
but this building's heating and air system is unpredictable,
and I mustn't complain, must wear shiny black heels and a pink sweater set,
professional and cheery like my mother the accountant,
like, "Thank you for coming today,"
"This bright orange booklet details your rights,"
"Please bear with me as I adhere to the script,"
and, "Do you have any questions?"

PIGMENT
Angie Marie Gonzalez

They want to wear your skin
They don't want to live in it
They don't want you to live in it

KNOWING
Hil Hoover

I know there is life inside me.
I know there is life inside me
Because every pulse point is a riot
Because I have become all
Windtunnel ears and whirlpool throat
Because each heartbeat has become
The cave of echoes from my childhood
Carrying voices from afar so very clearly.
I know there is life inside me
Because every vertebra is shatterspark
Every muscle is clutchstrain
Every breath is slow rattlesnake warning
Of an unavoidable fate
Because I have become in this moment
Not greenblue ocean as I have styled myself
But warning light house fire emergency red.
I know there is life inside me
Because on a night when the
Desperate scramble to get the pain levels down
- long bath good scents nsaids rest now
water down resistant throat and food slowly relished
rub here stretch there -
has failed miserably
I am still here, writing.

DISTILLED ESSENCE OF STARDUST
Michael Sindler

CONTENTS: Human Being/ Adult
(Distilled Essence of Stardust)
SERVING SIZE: 1
SERVINGS PER CONTAINER: 1
NUTRITIONAL FACTS: (AVERAGE)
CALORIES: 110,000
TOTAL FAT: 15-40% BMI
SODIUM: 210 gm.
PROTEIN: 20% by wt.
NET WEIGHT: Varies
INGREDIENTS:

Oxygen	0.65
Carbon	0.18
Hydrogen	0.10
Nitrogen	0.03
Calcium	0.014
Phosphorus	0.011

ALSO CONTAINS IN TRACE AMOUNTS:
Potassium, Sulfur, Sodium, Chlorine,
Magnesium, Iron, Fluorine, Zinc, Silicon,
Rubidium, Strontium, Bromine, Lead, Copper,
Aluminum, Cadmium, Cerium, Barium, Tin,
Iodine, Titanium, Boron, Selenium, Nickel,
Chromium, Manganese, Arsenic, Lithium, Mercury,
Cesium, Molybdenum, Germanium, Cobalt,
Antimony, Silver, Niobium, Zirconium, Lanthanum,
Tellurium, Gallium, Yttrium Bismuth, Thallium, Indium,
Gold, Scandium, Tantalum, Vanadium, Thorium, Uranium,
Samarium, Tungsten, Beryllium, and Radium

NOT A SIGNIFICANT SOURCE OF:
Common Sense, Ability to Protect Planet,
Agreement with Others
PRODUCED BY: Random Coupling
DISTRIBUTED BY: Random Factors
Including: Economics, Climate, Political Instability

QUALITY GUARANTEE: None
DO NOT USE AFTER EXPIRATION DATE
NOT FROM CONCENTRATE

GETTING OLD IS HELL!
Navita Gunter

Listen up young people and listen well!
While the Golden years of aging has its perks
It can also be HELL!
Like when you begin to have aches and pains that you never
Felt before!
And you have to think TWICE because of your back and knees
Before bending down to try and pick up something off
The floor!
Or when your eyes begin to play tricks on you!
And you start to not see as far or near as you used to!
And your mind makes finding things more challenging like
 an endless game of clue!
When you wake up from a really HARD night's sleep and you find
That you seemed to have been beaten and bruised all black and blue!
Like someone had taken a stick and gone to town on you!
When you start to develop intimate and ongoing relationships
With doctors that in your YOUTH you never knew existed!
Now, you have them on your phone's speed dial like your closest
 family and friends so you can immediately get drug and hospital care
assistance!

Yes, children, getting old can be HELL! That is true,
But, the alternative is NOT! Getting old!
Well, I think that I will pass on that for now
 wouldn't YOU!?

BUGGED OUT
Christine Hall

Hours after the performance, I stand before the mirror in my dressing room and
     reflect.
The dressing room is my bathroom and I only use it to undress.
My yoga teacher was an actor.
He called our bodies costumes. I digress to redress my wounded ego.
Two to tango, two leads in this play. Hours later, alone, I interrogate
each line for new meaning, pouring over every pore
squeezing out information, clues, cues, critique, catharsis
inserting alternate scenes, sequences, endings, practiced as dramatic
     reenactments.
Vindicated in this monologue, and better prepared for the role of Frankenbug.

You make me act like a monster in this loopy head movie
where no one speaks to what's really happening.
What we're thinking and feeling are the aces up our sleeves.
My great-great-great grandfather lost our hometown in a card game.
There's a school named for him, they're living lessons
in near dead languages. Monster is Latin as any old grey notion.
Monstrare: to show, what a show we put on.
Monstrum: to warn, I warned you what could go wrong.

I've got the bug to improv Frankenstein, mould and improve my face
recount his bride, intercut and erase
punch holes in my ears, nine on one side
with rings that were extracted by forceps when we rolled
three and a half times. The doctor presented the fragments
in a test tube trophy. There were forceps in the delivery room
and a cast of understudies awaiting
baby, these are tweezers and I'm pulling the ace out of my sleeve
to win this wager against Frankenbug inside me.

Hours later our conversation's still bugging me.
I pluck each of the bugs I placed earlier carefully
as I lean over the sink and contemplate, these loops replay on repeat.
Earworms rally through my brain. I exhume the remains of our exchange
perform the opposite of an autopsy, reconstructing the scene, maggots feast
and bugs crawl all over me. I'm made of bugs.
I'm Frankenbug, assembled to avenge
the segments that were sentenced to premature deaths.

Hours later, two usually, when I'm craving a cigarette
I rehearse for next time awaiting callback.
My hand goes in again and it's too late to play anything but solitaire,
show my face, get stoned enough, drunk as Baudelaire
in Belgium. I level with my smoke streaked eyes
framed in swollen red curtains, stuck in the spotlight.
When I am ready to face you as I am then I will ace the audition.

THE HOLES I HAVE
Henry L. Jones

A soft light reflects
on my walls filling the room
with cheerful, dancing silhouettes
images tracing along hidden places
flood my brain through these holes
in my head called eyes.

These strange creatures soar through
the pinks, blues & whites of the covers
quilted happiness to the strands and stories
heard each night of places and people
then warm kisses good-night echo in my mind
through the holes in my head called ears.

Now old drinking brandy full-bodied
a calm invades my bones with warmth
bringing a hush, a contentment like those stories
drinking nectar to rain on the castles in my mind
playful games kill the dragon flowing inside
through the long gutter in my head called a mouth.

Years of the living, the dead, the hushed, the moving,
ancient winds blow across my face scent of old lies
Becoming a dry desert once salty oceans of plenty
aromas persist along the flowing currents
rye from the fields, roses on the bush, strings of honeysuckle
through these downward holes in my head called a nose.

The sights, sounds, tastes and smell of you from those years
surrounding me inspiring me to paint an unseen image
many pictures replayed and relived but longing for you
those things which I have yet to see or feel for many years
I peeked back at those moments wondering what to do now
with the hole in my chest where a heart once pounded for you.

TORRENTIAL
Dennis Stefanov

I had always studied the features on earth's skin
comparing them to symbols of language
that we used to teach each other
     about what lies beneath the surface

we would walk over
subterranean rivers
on stone, dirt, leaves, and grass
snapping branches from trees
right underneath our feet
their echoing obscenities carried off
     split by razor-like winds

underneath parting clouds after rain
you called me a beam of sunlight
illuminating your normally half-
crooked smile, and heavy eyes

eyes that seemingly wandered
whenever mine seamlessly followed
the curves of your figure
discovering recently unearthed tributaries
on your thighs

pouring yourself onto me
we always wondered if people
carved into the earth
to try digging for themselves
     you were just more curious

I remember following a red river
        to the bathtub faucet
I heard the roar of a torrent,
        spilling over porcelain edges
pooling on the tile floor
        but what does it mean
        when you cannot tell the difference
between blood and water

Intimate Inhumanities
Rhoda Thomas

Her screams reached all the way from the room where they did it
All the way down the motorway and through the months of worry
Until I sit in the waiting-room, waiting for my turn.

Perhaps she hurt the first time she ever opened her legs to someone
Not quite like the magazines had said
Maybe, even then, she cried and sunk her nails in
and begged him to stop.

But I have insulated myself in paperwork
Considered the patient testimonies, some good some bad,
read the health board evaluations, the savings in time and money
The 'gold standard' for safety much preferred to knocking us out cold.
I know on balance this is the best way to do it.

Maybe she didn't have her first sex
in a student flat, *Dark Side of the Moon*
Chenille cushions, flickering candlelight.
Maybe it was a relative when she was too young
or a young boy too clumsy and eager to stop
or maybe she learned to thrust and writhe and kick
whenever something was bad.
Maybe she didn't learn to silence herself,
to please, appease, tease
Maybe the more she screamed,
the more she hoped something would change.

The waiting room is stark, bleached, laminated instructions on the walls
Seats cordoned off because of the virus
No one else here, just the echoes of women before me
Some who cried, some who wouldn't let themselves.

Women who've never heard of the *Villa Grimaldi*
Women who've never allowed the knowledge of torture to penetrate their
    consciousness
Women who don't know that sisters everywhere
Are suffering intimate inhumanities
at the hands of guards, police, fellow prisoners, on camera
for just being ...
a Buddhist
a resident in a poor community
a doctor treating a wounded protestor
the wife of a Muslim man
someone who posted something critical on facebook
someone who thinks differently.

What do we mean by solidarity?
What do we mean by solidarity?

I've insulated myself in paperwork
The academic studies, the statistics
Believing the science.
Believing the politics.

Today, there will be no electric shocks.
No brooms or sticks or bottles or canes.

Today I will think of you and the beautiful sex we had
When the opening of self was something I gave to you
When it was the route to building what we share
When I stopped disconnecting from sorrow
And tears of happiness pricked at the edge of my eyes.

75

The clock ticks in the waiting-room
They call me,
but it's just to take my blood pressure,
to weigh me,
to check my date of birth.
Really, it's OK.
The flex will be very thin.
They will use anaesthetic.
They are kind.

FAWN
Beady Man

The misery of her life
Is etched in her eyes
No close ties,
Just a series of goodbyes,

What holds her here,
Tears her apart,
The haze helps her forget
Where did it all start?

A mysoginist's dream
Just an object to lie on,
A punching bag for her pimp,
With no-one to rely on.

She moved here to escape,
the hand she was dealt,
Glazed eyes now, arm outstretched,
teeth clutching a belt,

Sweet relief
Just moments away,
But tomorrow,
Won't be just another day.

Long ago she lost her dreams,
Along with her fight,
Ain't no time for fantasies,
Reality bites,

The things that she's endured,
Over the last year,
Are more than anyone,
Should be asked to bear,

She fled her hometown,
To escape the abuse,
Just to find herself,
Once again being used,

Bright lights, Big City,
This ain't no fairytale existence,
working 14 hour days,
At the end left with a pittance,

Collapsed veins, frail limbs,
Point to the way that she's living,
battered and bruised,
These streets are unforgiving.

Was just a few weeks back,
She had a backstreet abortion,
Fight or flight for her,
Just ain't an option,

She's built up debts,
There's only one way she can pay,
Filthy floors, dirty alleys,
Selling her soul everyday,

She thought he loved her,
As he slowly drew her in,
Weed, Coke, then Crack,
Now all she craves is Heroin,

A continuous cycle,
She has nowhere to go,
To her aggressor,
She's just a dirty whore,

Features gaunt and skeletal,
Body close to broken,
Eyes deep set,
And voice softly spoken,

And you'll see this girl's story,
Is so fucking obscene,
As tomorrow,
She'll turn fifteen.

LIFE MACHINE
Markey Mark Symmonds

I know you are there, all I can do is stare at the inside of my mind. I'm still alive, to tell you I strive, but, I can't make you see I'm still alive. No movement I make, you hope I awake, laying here is not the person you know, I look like a fake. Tears in your eyes as you start to cry fearing that I have died. I feel you squeeze my hand, I want to squeeze back but I'm paralyzed, trying to find a way back.

This wretched machine keeps humming, keeping this piece of debris running, wires and tubes from my body protrude, my life support, my food. I've seen the light, the tunnel of flight, but I have fought to stay here with all my might. I want to tell you I'm alright, that I will continue the fight until I can be with you again tucked up in the moonlight.

I still see the day and know everything you say and do, I'm watching everyone and every move, I know how you feel, how the kids are, I even know you banged the car. I wish I could open my eyes and see where you are.

Days of rolling around in my own brain, powerful drugs that kill the pain, it's driving me insane. In my mind, I wrote a poem for you, I hope one day I will be able to read it aloud too. I see you are weary, you need sleep too, come lay with me until the day is new.

THIGHS
Hil Hoover

Even when hissed by a viper
Words can be true
Yes my thighs have served as destination or pathway
For any number of tongues or hands, cunts or cocks,
But that has never been a secret I tried to keep

The part that you seem to misunderstand
Is that those imperfect scarred surfaces
Might serve as pathways or destinations
Might be used with or without permission, leaving bruises or kiss marks
    or broken skin
But what they are, what defines their existence
Their clench and release, their rocking motion, their faltering weakness at
    the end of a long day,
their strength in lifting, in holding, in standing,
Is only in relation to my use, my path, my movement.

ASH
Dane Ince

Supernova fucking
Hot goddamn hot
Tsunami earthquakes in the garden rolling over spent okra bushes
Stinging nettles aching for the itching
More more begging for more
It is so bad
We have to scream god oh god
Like we hate the agony we love
We cannot help ourselves ending ocean in heaps
Beasts silent for a moment dreaming
That might be you
That might be me
Sitting in the corner
Reverting to the safety
Of the smallness
Beaten into me
That could be me with the dimming of light
No need to worry
This was fucked up long before the curtain went up
No need for guilt
No need for pity
It's just me hobbling off
On what is left of stumps
Leaving a trail
Of bloody pus
I am drawing a blank on the ending
That is a convenient lie
Recent and honest experience
Says tragically
How about making peace with that
Losing proposition so hard to take
Let's do anything let's just skate
Let's bury sadness in endless song
And dance to avoid what we know will be
The premonition straitjacket

Has all the magic eight ball answers
Verifiable by planchette
Sigh oh endless sigh
I will right this ship
If
All that remains from the crashing on rock in the fog
Is nothing but a mere bundle of sticks

I love you
As I must have always loved you
I read the history
And it is the same every time though
Fatal tragic
Bleeding for the chance of a moment of bliss
Transient
In ancient rhyme lore
I think all kinds of things
Barricades to not allow for feeling
Bending stretching no dreaming my dead body snoring
Were these the trifles of gods and goddesses
Do you have any idea of the crushing
The dead weight of you on my body
Of my wiping your ass
My lover's ass
Cleaning up your piss
Doctoring your diaper rash
And seeing the beautiful curl in your pubic hair
Knowing I will never cum inside you again
You sleep in a box now
Your body ash
I stroke your thighs
Play with your nipples and breasts
So much beach sand now running through fingertips
I lick a finger pick up some of your beautiful ash body
I suck you off my finger

Swallow and now your body is inside my body
Finally, as close as we will ever be again
For as long as we may spin around the sun

BREATHING
Meg Smith

Eyes of the desert
I plead your silence,
your knowing beneath
a sash of gauze —
petals dither on a hot wind.
The syllables fall,
as we draw, closer,
unhidden, face to face.

Sorry
Michael Collins

I was sexually abused as a child
Collateral damage
I suffered physical abuse when young
Collateral damage
I have anger management issues
Collateral damage
I have a short fuse
Collateral damage
I lost control
Collateral damage

She drove me to it
Collateral damage
She had an affair
Collateral damage
She left and took the kids
Collateral damage
She left me with nothing
Collateral damage

I have my pride
Collateral damage
I was made to feel small
Collateral damage

She needed to be taught a lesson
Collateral damage
She would not give me sex
Collateral damage
She was being a bitch
Collateral damage

I never learned how to act responsibly in life
I was not adequately socialized
I had severe psychological trauma growing up
I have an inadequate personality and low self-esteem
I have mental health issues

I am a victim here too!

There is a war inside my head!

Unintended consequences! I didn't mean it! Collateral damage!

"I am sorry"

Sorry…?

'Sorry' doesn't cut it… mate!

UNWELCOME HOUSEGUEST
Leslie Shakira Garcia

Womanhood is an unwelcome houseguest.
It's 3am–she's stopped by for a cup of sugar and my innocence.

I lock the door on mother nature, close the blinds, stay perfectly still for
twenty minutes, and make my breaths shallow.

I morph into my abuelita when she's trying to hide from Jehovah's
witnesses.

Womanhood rings the doorbell again, realizes I am the only one home,
and sets my life ablaze.

Unbecoming child at age 12 is like learning your house is on fire.

The photo albums of your childhood burned by a new body shape. The
rooftops of your self-esteem up in flames. The door knobs of your skin,
once cool to touch, now blistering to feeling.

I was taught to stop, drop, and roll.

But never to stop comparing my body to photoshopped magazine covers
and television screens.

Never taught to drop the stigma of showing "too much" skin. When did
skin become sin?

Taught to roll away from my emotions because it was my "time of the
month." When did body fluids invalidate feelings?

I remember getting cat-called before I ever got my first period.

I learned how to hate my body, before I ever knew it deserved love.
I weighed myself every day in the eighth grade because that is where
young girls like me found value.

We yelled mantras into the wind like, "I must, I must, I must increase my bust,"

My friends blossomed while I continued in my devoted prayer,

"Are you There God? It's me, your just and faithful servant who has the bust of a twelve-year-old boy."

Puberty was supposed to be a metamorphosis to turn this Ugly Betty into Sofia Vergara. I'm still waiting.

There are stories in our homeland of women getting beaten to death by their husbands, because they deserved it.

A madman's rage justified by machismo and a village.

They tell of young girls in school-uniforms being robbed of their innocence in the dusty back roads behind their houses,

Rape justified by clothing choices and a village.

Mankind has been blaming women for its fall since the genesis of creation, as if we forced man to eat the fruit of wisdom.

Mankind has been stepping on women, as if we came from the sole of their feet and not the side of their rib.

History makes man hero while making woman cause of death, cause of war, or cause of damnation.

It's 3 am, she's come by for a cup of sugar and my innocence.

When I finally let mother nature in, I realize womanhood is not enemy but destiny.

Standing in the flames, I allow the light to engulf me.

In unbecoming child, I no longer see myself as something to be extinguished.

It is the first time I look in the mirror and see my mother's halo of a smile in my reflection.

Womanhood has always been an unwelcome houseguest,
But I'm learning to make comfort out of this uncomfortable body.

BODY SNATCHERS
Caroline Minter

I stay in SILICON Valley
Where I have to TUCK my TUMMY as I travel to and fro
Sometimes I must LIFT my FACE
In order to face the world and grow

My HAIR is another dimension
Being chased by TRANSPLANTS and EXTENSIONS

I try to stay aBREAST
Sometimes it takes me up
And sometimes it takes me down
Because you know LIPO sucks the life out of you
But you gotta do what you gotta do
        BUTT
BOTOX is my best friend,
We'll be together till the end
CELLULITE was like a twin
Till I treated her I had to defend
Myself that is
You know, in order to live

Ran into old RHINO being NOSEy as usual you see
So I had to get a CHEMICAL and PEEL him off of me
                    and

CHIN was my friend who liked to lift weights
Constantly on the RESHAPE
Make you do a double take
Ended up being FAKE
        BUTT
Now I'm finally free
Many changes to many degrees
It's all said and done
And it wasn't cheap Hun

MY BODY IS SNATCHED   !!!!

IT'S A BEAUTIFUL DAY, MOMMY
Amanda Oliver Hendricks

A shower every few days
will save your life.
Even if you can't stand
long enough to run water
through the "S" of your stretch marks.
Jesus, you have learned to walk on slime.
No time for clean tubs
your body wants to collapse
but your mother's intuition
is too stubborn to release
the muscles overprotecting
a tailbone shattered into pieces
after more than twelve hours
of labor.
Too exhausted
to brush your teeth
you blame the draining mucus
gifted by the green-goblin two year old
for the rankness of breath.
Praise the God of imagination
your son has recently fallen
in fanboy with dragons.
Tonight he says there is a fire-breather outside
puts a pudgy finger over his lips
It's asleep, he whispers.
I pray
this tiny prophet cut from my insides
bloody and screaming
does indeed
know how to keep dragons
still
asleep
quiet.
It's dark in here.
He tells his Daddy.

Turn on the light.
He doesn't know how to flip the switch alone.
Some days
neither do I.

My crotch smells like hamsters.
I confess
to my husband.
He has long hair
again
has taken to wearing t shirt scraps
stained with coffee
to push back unwashed, matted curls.
He is now our savior.
My gooch smells like buttered popcorn.
He replies.
These words
alone
are more
true love than a misspelled tattoo
or a full-priced Whitman's Sampler
purchased before Valentine's Day.
He makes ice packs for my honey pot
refuses to look
at the photo I managed to "selfie"
of my "situation"
having seen my hot pocket explode
into a large black hole live.
Yes, my flower now flaps
like Pop Pop's booty cheeks
on a good old man fart day
but our love grew a new baby to hold
beautiful and squishy
who will be acne reddened and potty-mouthed too fast
hopefully never knowing

he was conceived
on a night mommy was tired
and daddy afraid
she would be mad
if he slid the condom on himself.

The smell of baby
spit up
sound of green pudding poops pouring
into overpriced diapers
are more than enough to keep
communication deficits distant.
I had the doctor sew my skin and sinew back together
in the shape of letters
L   O   V   E
It is why he is so strong,
why I have to pee
four times standing
over the drain
during a thirty minute shower.

SOUR
Patricia Alice Albrecht

My malaise –
more morning sickness
than menopause
alerts – queasy with questions
bloated – bungled
incubating indecision
over miscarried memories

if I let my guard down
will my colonic collisions
rush forth,
call foul against my ego?

Once upon a time
gestations were fairytales
full of happily ever afters.

I was Goldilocks
among the bears
looking for ways to feed my heart

as Cinderella I toiled
to help juggle other's dreams

a Beauty Sleeping
I woke to see
the chrone, Baba Yaga
reflecting in the mirror

like my mother
she waves an arthritic finger
raises an eyebrow
says something fecund
but her breath fogs the answers.

Is this the fatigued
first trimester of
activated death
or could I be...
am I pregnant
with all
that is becoming
of me?

WINDOW
Patricia Alice Albrecht

"If I had gone down to the frog pond and really listened to the frogs...
Perhaps I could have recognized in myself what they were feeling."
–Galway Kinnell, from his interview by Bill Moyers in
The Language of Life

"When we don't see the self as self what do we have to fear?" –The Tao

From behind my glass wall
I cannot hear
the birds chitter and fluff
flitting from feeders
to snow pocked
with pecks and claws.

I cannot hear
the Junco's black-backed poem
the Dove's small-beaked discontent
or the Starlings swoop to steal it all.

It's the wind's crescendo
thru the orchestra of dogwood branches
cracked and tinkling in thaw
the cymbals of smashed icicles
that calls me
      calls me
            calls me
                  outside
this lock-down
I've named
Self.

SPIRIT

SACRAL
Kana Kavon

some Souls must roam the ocean floor womb of the world where
land and water deny their differences here
Ancestors stretch into new skins.
some Souls must settle here
and not fear
bones walking
skulls wailing
teeth gnashing
the loss of life
and light
as we have known them.
some Souls must know hell
in order to tell
the living.

ABOVE THE MANTLE
Nina Adel

A baby
was found between the wooden shards,
beneath muddy walls in ruins
perched in irrational safety
on a bright blue bucket
over traces of soiled ocean
in a clean pink teddy-bear suit,
blinking and cold and living

an ancient man
was found
on a roof on the surface of the ocean
protected by the inverted reality
of the house he'd built
expecting water from above
as his adversary

a jailed man
was never found

a girl running from the erupting core
of her father's anger
was never found

a mother bent before the kitchen altar
in a pressed blue suit
kneeling on her son's yellow schoolbag
was never found

a pair of middle-aged lovers
laughing on the floor
atop abandoned blankets
was never found

a stiffened body in a dedicated room
awaiting its own reduction
was never found

a thousand bodies
drowned before half the world awakened
were never found.

Is there,
somewhere inside
my older life,
a baby,
unexpected
between the wooden shards,
blinking and cold and living
borne along, unlikely and protected on a wave
radiating outward from the brutal shift
in the tectonic plates
that are scraping and flowing
pausing recklessly on the surface
of my own asthenosphere?

THE INDIE MOVIE ABOUT MY FATHER
Carl Lowe

When I think about my visits to
My father in the hospital during his series of strokes
that eventually killed him I picture them
as a black and white Indie movie
Low budget. Dialogue is mostly improv.
Long uncomfortable silences
Fantasy scenes where I'm
staring into one of the abandoned
closets in my father's house,
filled with stacks of papers, empty bottles,
boxes of chalk, scrapbooks
filled with the strange pictures my
father took of the family.
The plot of the movie is roundabout, circular
never arriving at a definite turning point,
maybe interrupted with flashbacks.
I could show the afternoon, while I was running
for the New York State House of Representatives
I was at lunch with people supporting my campaign
and a woman at the lunch realizes that my father had been her
son's elementary school teacher. She told me
that my father saved her son's life. Her son's outlook
had been crashing, depressed, bored, destructive
but something about my
father's insane love of fantasy had sparked
her son into finding a purpose
and getting a grip on things he loved.
And then we could view a version of
that afternoon on the two lane blacktop near
the Baseball Hall of Fame in Cooperstown New York
my father asleep at the wheel in that
van he drove, my mother asleep in the front
passenger seat beside him
a car behind them honking wildly, a panicked driver trying
to wake my father as the van veered back and

103

forth across the two lane road
from one side of the road to the other
like the gyrating needle on a boiler
about to explode.
And a young unsuspecting woman, a former beauty pageant winner
I would read later
nine months pregnant driving down
that fatal road toward my parents
exploding into
one of those
awful crashes
a violent three seconds
followed by deathly silence
where only the driver who's
at fault survives.
The police officer writing up the
traffic report afterwards classified the
head on collision as non-survivable
and I know my sense of well-being
certainly didn't survive it.
But as the crushed cars
sat in their hieroglyphic twists
of metal and plastic
my father stumbled
out of the van, walking dazed away from
the flattened cars and flattened lives
with only a couple of broken ribs.
Later he complained to me about the rough way
the first responders had dragged my
mother's body from the
twisted vehicles.
Of course, the rough way the families of the dead
were dragged from their daily lives
they had presumed made sense
and woke in their new nightmare

about that my father had nothing to say.
Oh, Dad's lawyer got him off
with some
sort of lawyerly sleight of hand I could
almost understand. That legal magic
trick incensed the local folks
around Cooperstown who grieved
the dead almost-mother and her lifeless fetus.
And Dad came to live with me after that
in one of those surreal suburbs
where I was living where everyone
pretends they're living the American dream. So every day
I would ride the commuter train to the corporate
dog-eat-dog high profile magazine job where ad agency
people constantly tried to bribe me to run stories
about their products and I could eat for free
at any restaurant in New York City and I would treat
my scruffy writer friends to lunch at ridiculously high class
insanely overpriced restaurants. Then at night
I'd come back home to Dad, my wife and three
kids.
My father's way of grieving and feeling guilty was…
well I'm still trying to understand it or grasp it.
But it's elusive, the way he always was.
After the crash, he didn't live with us long, seemed to be in a hurry
to move back to his empty house, find a new girlfriend
and do his daily denial meditations, saluting each new
day like a dream that requires no backstory, but contains
naked events that signify what can't
be identified.
The movie I'm making in my head would have
his first stroke.
He's asleep at home,
a fire starts in his living room in the fireplace
and his house filled with his hoarding treasures

is soon ablaze.
He escapes out a first floor window
as the empty aerosol cans that fill the hallway
begin to explode.
His feet touch the grass outside
the window and he has a vision.
In the vision he's the secret man
who runs the world. The politicians, the CEOs,
the celebrities all visit him for
advice. He's in bed telling them
the truth about how the world really works,
and how to beat the system.
And when he opens his eyes he is in bed, a hospital
bed, after the stroke, lecturing me on how the world
really works and how to outwit the world's manipulators.
And the lectures become a series of
talks, meandering, mostly gibberish
interrupted by each stroke.
And I keep visiting for the next lecture
until one day, still in the hospital,
he falls asleep and never wakes up.

The last thing I remember him saying to me
before his eyes closed that last time was that
the head of the Federal Reserve, Alan Greenspan,
didn't know what he was doing.
Although I have to admit they were the type of last words
you don't forget I don't think my father ever got to the
part about exactly what Alan Greenspan
should have been doing.
At my father's funeral I overheard my uncle
arguing with my sister about my cousin,
my uncle's son who lives in California. My uncle was insisting that
he didn't have a son.
Exactly why my uncle suddenly

claimed his son didn't exist…
no one could ever explain that to me.
At my father's funeral I had the sense
that his spirit was still restless, not at peace.
There was commotion coming from
Dad's spirit, a need to still beat the system,
set the world straight, finally explain
how the world really worked. Unable to accept
the idea that maybe the world didn't really
work at all.
After the services for my father and the burial, my uncle
said something to me about my father's
days playing college football.
That was news to me. My father
had never mentioned it to me. Ever.
Of course now that generation is all dead –
my father, my uncle, the lawyer who
got my father off, all my parent's friends.
So as the movie slips toward the end
Maybe I'd cut to that afternoon
in Cullman, Alabama when after an afternoon nap
I sat up and a ghost drifted into
the room flowing across the bed at
a 45 degree diagonal.
It said it had an important
message for me
and then kept on drifting into
nothingness never
finishing the thought.
Then I'd roll the credits,
perhaps roll them across
the screen, the landscape
in the background a little blurry,
slightly out of focus.

GOOD GRIEF
Gabby White

I am a lousy weapon with much less effect
I won't tell you what caused me to get this way
the cotton quilt says its prayer every night as I lie awake to bear witness
"need you not, I curl up to play dead just in case"
and I dare not compare this illuminated city that bleeds side-winding
    highways of comfort
to the weight of you lying next to me

worn out soldier turned lover, you brought me saints' sleep
one look changed definitions of how I'm supposed to be seen
never stopping me from significantly winning all of my own arguments
harmonizing space between what I know and what I thought I knew
you said you watch the art of hand gesture, a body language I didn't speak
    before
now I know how to hold myself in this body since it's the only place I can
    be when I can't touch
yours

I may not know you really
but good grief I love what I know when I think about loving you
I know capability wading back and forth between who's most guilty
what do I know that you cannot teach me
what happens when newborns grow up empty
to find fulfillment in someone else's body

KIRSCHNER'S GROOVY STYLE
Jeff Cottrill

Kirschner wasn't like the others. Oh no. He had his own style. He followed his own vibe. He was a lone werewolf marching to the tune of his own cellist, out in centre field with the shortstops and the running backs, an odd man in with the *enfants horribles*, if you catch the jib of my drift. Kirschner had a groovy style, and none of his colleagues could match it. He thought they were all suckers. Squares. Conformist slaves. Gutless wonders stuck between a rut and a hard drive, if you feel the lick of my hat.

"Cats, you got to adopt a groovier style like me," he told his colleagues every day. "That's why you don't stand out. That's why you blend into the background with all the bugs and the rocks and the stuff. See, when you got a groovy style like mine, you don't need to waste no time with *preparation*. You don't need to plan ahead when you trust in your skills and knowledge. You don't need to put on no mask or wear no protective equipment or even wash your hands. You just dive right into it and move with the flow in your head, Fred."

And his colleagues would always stare at him with dumbfounded faces, their small, petty minds unable to grasp the grooviness of his style, if you catch the grunt of my hogweed. One was always sure to say, "But you really should wash your hands before you begin, Dr. Kirschner," or something like that, but he never let it faze him. His buzz was too strong to burst from such cold, dull logic.

"Fellow babies," he would say, "when you got a groovy style like mine, you don't need a plan, Stan. You don't need a course of action, Jackson. You don't need a map... Plap. You don't even need to know the nature of the patient's illness. Why? Why tone down your buzz with such a snooze fest? Just trust in your soul, slice 'im open, stick your hands in the goo and do what feels right."

And that's what Kirschner did every time. All patients got the same treatment, whether they were expecting a heart transplant or an appendectomy – Kirschner saw every one of them as a pure equal, if you get the nuts of my Rolodex. Everybody got a taste of the Kirschner groove, whether his colleagues approved or not.

"Surgery, man," he always said, bobbing his head from side to side with a saucy grin. "Surgery. Don't ever let The Man tell you it's a cold, precise discipline that needs years of study and practice. The Man's lyin' to you. Surgery's an art form, Norm. You gotta feel your way into it. You gotta listen to your muse. You gotta let the vibe of the room dictate where you're gonna go. I only listen to the vibe. If the vibe tells me, 'Third lung,' I'm slappin' a third lung on the mother, no matter what the squares say. Vibe tells me, 'Man, that spleen, it ain't jivin' with my beat,' you can bet your little hiney I'm tearin' out that spleen and eatin' it raw for dinner. Vibe tells me, 'The world is ripe for some... experimentation,' man, you never know what you're gonna wake up with. If the muse orders me to, I will turn your face into a literal Picasso painting. See, I don't give a horse's funny bone about the rules, Jules. I don't have to follow 'convention.' Surgery's not a job. Surgery's not a profession. Surgery... is an adventure."

And it was an adventure that many lucky souls shared with Kirschner, if you catch the lump of my hasenpfeffer, if you get the stern of my arrow, if you know the grunt of my Clampett. So the next time you're walking down your local boulevard, and you spot a man with five ears, or a lady with no neck, or a horse with no name, or just a cemetery, you will know you're looking at the fruits of Kirschner's groovy style.

MY LATE HUSBAND'S CLOTHES
Meg Smith

Some summer days,
we'd pass men on the street,
in a bivouac of towels and folding chairs.
He'd give them money, sunglasses.
The time came when I opened the closet.
curating — jackets that crossed the
Upper Peninsula wilderness,
boots that crunched dry leaves
at the top of Frankenstein Cliff.
On many streets, and many mountains,
his threads are covering an army of poets,
his sunglasses shading eyes, empty of tears.
We are all gathered, by the docks,
as cars glide past. Voices rise to the
moon — half-shaded, but whole.

AUTUMN'S ANGUISH
P W Lea

Autumn's Anguish / To again die all over
Stretching out exhausted / Slumped into the backseat
Nervous about stain, / Dirt, whereas the smell of it.
Catching us on every step / So we took them /
Two at a time. / Enough time of crayons coloring the
Walls / With childish exaggerations / So blessed were we /
That we hung out solemnly / Mad at what were / Stupid
Enough to believe / That you were going to be a dancer /
And a singer too if they would listen / That they already
Had / all the words / all the moves / "Study," I said. /
You grinned / It didn't make any difference /
This indifference to / My old man / Your old man /
All the old men's words decay into they didn't make it. /
But we made it. / On a mud trample foyer /
Naked a straining before the collapse of the sun /
In one melding arch / The world was young /
Stubborn and laughing / Our will was creation being done.
They said you died in the fall / Slow starling start /
They said you had a baby, and in pieces cried that
I should share the pain. / They said you were a dancer
In Chattanooga / but did not like the weather / Whether
Or not they ever listen to what you say. Aged beneath
The cancelled out months of an orange Autumn calendar.

GREEN
Ray Zimmerman

In the dead of winter, the leafless trees mock death.
The body of mother earth seems to be a corpse,
until you arrive, embodiment of springtime.

Goddess or Green Man, androgynous figure,
the earth is renewed when you appear.
The green of springtime reflects your skin.

I search for Oberon and Titania in your headdress
of boulders and rising vapors as they dream elsewhere.
They await the bard's call for it is not yet midsummer's eve.

The swimmers dive into your private ocean
just as they appeared in Whitman's poems,
Poet of the fecund earth he would appreciate
your presence surrounded by vines and shrubs.

In your vernal appearance I contemplate my age,
the mystery that I am still here after so many years.
The cycle of seasons will bring you back again,
but a man's life is linear, physical existence transitory.
My spirit will be here to greet you, but my body may not.

THE BREVITY OF ONENESS
Regan Smith

I know that my soul is separate
from my body, for there are times
where my body continues to move,
continues to breathe but my soul
is three steps removed, overlooking
this body from a bird's eye view.

It controls this drone of legs and
arms and eyes, moving its gaze from
left to right–to smile at a stranger,
or the footing's next step–
but my feelings are locked and
sprouted within this soul, detached
from the bones and muscles.

I wonder if my body and soul will
ever marry, for they've been
separate for quite some time,
allowing the brevity of oneness:

for the duration of a dance,
for my mother's embrace,
for the exhilarating jump from
plane high–temporarily united
as we soar through air, falling
through clouds, occupying the
space that's only meant for:
the amakihi,
the white-tailed tropicbird,
the golden plover.

My body gets bathed,
but my soul can still hold shame.

My spirit can be filled
and overflowing,
yet the peach figure I see
is in languish with night
still ringing around her eyes.

And I know that my body,
will fall to the earth,
decompose and wrap itself with
the roots,

but my soul will soar,
for it has shed its weight,
and reunited with the
totality of eternity.

HEROIN (A LIFE CYCLE)
Reese North

Delusion:
>An illusion
>which escapes the censor of the eyes
>becomes a delusion between the ears.

Betrayal:
>Yesterday is so many memories,
>tomorrow, just a junkie's promise.

Overdose:
>'Now pass the pick and set me free
>I'll be gone along my way
>and you'll forget
>those broken windows in my head.'

Passing:
>'Death stands silent by his gate
>while I gape at his open jaws
>Spy a star that beckons me
>to enter Evermore.'

Sermon:
>Heroin is a slut!
>   a cold cold whore,
>She'll jab you with her witch's finger
>   hold you by his warlock's eye
>Fuck you if you're not careful
>   bleed your heart until it's dry
>Twist you to his fork-tongued ways
>   take you where there's no more love:
>Taint you with her winter's touch
>Wed you withered until you're dust.

Empty.
Noel Marie

I tried to purge the worms out.
Instead I blew some out my nose.
I cannot let these worms stay in me.
Red rain dropped into the well.
I cannot find them.
They must be living within.
Thy body no longer thine.
Here they are.
Squirming around.
My home is not safe.
I must shower until I piss them out.
Or will I have to grab a knife and gut of the worms myself.
The worms may be in my mind.
I think about that sometimes.

SELF-PORTRAIT AS A PEACH PIT
Michelle Awad

All the boys come away with
chipped teeth.

Hard, uneven thing. Folds, like
a fingerprint you cannot trace,
bone-bent shell kissed by
fleshy pink.
The skin tears. The veil breaks.
You hold it, thumb and forefinger,
a new home, a fresh casing,
the only part you cannot digest
properly, the only morsel you
don't have permission
to taste.

The tangerine splits. The berry bleeds.
The peach lets you devour it
until

it doesn't.
Cyanide, and seed,
hard, uneven thing; a
flower blooming.
A stone at the center

of her being.

NAMES.
Serge Ray Rodrigo, Sergio Ramon Rodriguez, and Sir-Reyna Lucio

Sergio Ramon Rodriguez is a child.

That child's me…Hi.

I don't like talking, so…Bye. But…but; preschool scares me. The other kids don't like me. Because they don't wanna tear paper. I like making things outta paper. Like hats, and cats, and snow.

But I go away. And I watch "Winnie the Pooh" with my sister. I now miss her. I like how Eeyore puts the popped balloon in the empty honey pot. He made them both *not* useless, like me and my sister. Grandma says the "popped balloon" going in and out of the honey pot is just sex.

I don't know. So…wanna see me flex?! My sister can't walk…she can't talk…she can't make things outta paper. Then, Grandma couldn't do those things either.

Other kids can make things outta paper. So can mom and dad. They just don't wanna. They don't wanna, because they don't like me. I don't like me. So, mom says I'm like Eeyore. But Grandma says I'm the Cowardly Lion.

Serge Ray Rodrigo is the name the world bestowed upon me.

The world cannot pronounce *Sergio*. So, I let them shorten it to *Serge*. *Ray* is short for Ramon, my middle name. Plus, my sister used to call me *Ray*. *Rodrigo* is the root word for Rodriguez.

Rodrigo meant "famous power" and the "-ez" part…meant "follower of… Don Rodrigo." *Sergio* was originally Segunio…which meant guardian. Ramon meant "wise protection." So, when the world turned me into *Serge*, I was no longer a guardian.

So then, I chose *not* to follow "wise, famous, power."

I don't regret this. No one else believes that, but me.

One day, someone will wander into my midst. And they'll believe me. But deep down, I know this might not happen. So, I continue to be the keeper of order, the guardian of discipline, structure, logic, and reasoning. Not to mention the heart of science.

Until some cheese-perfumed person comes along and whispers in my ear, "You have no empathy."

Then, I whisper back, "you have no brain, Scarecrow. We're wandering around this planet-eating, making-more-humans, and defending-those-rights, by any means necessary...that's all there ever was...that's all there ever could be. Now, bow down to the Tin Man!"

I am derivative of my birth certificate. But *Serge Ray Rodrigo* must keep the order around here. When you talk to me at work, at the store, in public...I am *Serge*.

On social media, *Serge* reigns. *Serge* guards *Sergio*; even if that *means*... our names, no longer have meaning. *Serge* protects everyone from... from...*Sir-Reyna Lucio*.

Here they come now. Beware the charismatic, the enigmatic...the opaque.

Sir-Reyna Lucio is this fine-ass person you're looking at right here.

And fuck *Serge*. He thinks he's all bad with his long words and long sentences. I ain't the fuckin' Scarecrow, I beat his ass.

Why you looking all stupid?

Like I have my ass and tetas hanging out? Like my grandmother told me not to. I'm the *real* brains around here, *Sergio* is a little bitch. And *Serge* thinks he's so smart.

Pendejos.

They're in a relationship with penis on Facebook. I see them posing with it…

That's why they can't get no man. Not like me, I can get *any*one. My name is on the book we wrote. Without me, *Serge* can't type shit. They think they're so cool with their little Nirvana and "Ben" from that Michael Jackson rat movie.

They forget Carlos Santana is the only guy who *knows* us… That's the problem with the world…they act like they *knows* us.

Serge only gave me a name after he saw "Moonlight" two years ago… He's such a fake pendejo.

Sergio is better off with *me*.

> Our final voice lives in our inner silence. It only speaks to us in quotes.

"The only thing we have to fear…is fear of Nirvana," that was *kinda* from the end of "Cult of Personality" by Living Color. Or the voice starts singing… "Serge…the four of us need look no more…We've all found what we've been looking for!"

Or, it mimics some famous depressed character, "Nobody cares, about 'El Farol.' Nobody cares if we hold 'El Farol' high above our heads, like a lantern. Nobody cares about Santana, or my birthday."

But when our final voice speaks to you all…out loud…it doesn't sound like our inner voices. It's not just a Hispanic Latinx voice. It's a Black voice. It's a White voice, a *mixed* voice. It's an Immigrant and a Poverty voice. It's even a Disabled voice, and of course, a Feminine voice.

But most of all, it's our *inner* voice…destroying the silence of our friends. It's the outer silence that leads us to deeper conversation.

Our inner names…rhyme…with our children. For those are our names.

BEATS.
Sir-Reyna Lucio

Put your finger on our wrists, on our necks. Feel that beat?

Three races, 3 nationalities, 1 ethnicity, Africano Hispanic Latinx, this is how we feel the beat. The Bering Straight…the hard walk here…24,000 years ago.

Thousands of us die, all of us lost hope. Half of us left our old Gods behind in the stabbing cold. Three main migration waves, my people were the last. Feel that beat?

Grabbing slaves from Africa and hopping on a boat for a few months. That was easy. That had no beat…

Ozzy Osborne, banned from playing in Texas for pissing on the Alamo. He is always welcome as the true Prince of Darkness in Mexico forever! Davy Crockett and Daniel Boone can keep begging for all we care! Feel that beat?

Mexican or Asian…*squints*…Native American! That's another beat…

Super Street Fighter II comes out in the early 1990s. And there's a cool new character named T. Hawk. We feel that beat…

He wears a headdress of feathers and moccasins. And sits Indian style when he wins and says "how?" Other Native folks dance in the Mexican streets of his home stage. He uses attacks that mimic thunder birds and birds of prey. That's definitely a beat…

My black friends in Gary, Indiana, all single digit-aged, ask me why Street Fighter got T. Hawk's country wrong. He's from the USA, not Mexico. No beat. Can't feel that beat…

Later, my white Mexican mother rents West Side Story. And shows it to me and my sister for the first time. They love the songs and the romance. But my Puerto Rican father doesn't watch it. He tells us before leaving the room, "look at that brown makeup smeared all over those Italian actors! They didn't wanna find any real Puerto Ricans? And how the hell is gang violence in NY City romantic anyway?" Definite beat...two beats...three beats.

Years later, I learned about Chris Columbus killing Tainos with his bare hands in Puerto Rico. More years later, I learned about the Mexican American War that separated characters like T. Hawk...from people like me...my mother...the Mulatto slaves of Africano Hispanic Latinx sugar cane fields, like my grandfather and his father and his father. Beat...beat it like it's all or nothing...

It wasn't until a black boy punched me in the face for being a "white boy." Then, I understood that sometimes, we have even less place on this continent than expatriated black folks, who didn't even wanna come! I took that beat to the face. Because that made our pulse easier to find.

How to explain that to white people, without sounding racist against black people? Beat... How to explain that to black people, without sounding like complete aliens from another planet? Beat... How to explain that to reservation Native Americans, without sounding like one of them? Beat again...

Mystery Science Theater Comedian Jonah Ray's last name is Rodrigues... spelled with an "s" at the end. He told me, that makes him separate from me and my "z" at the end of my last name. He said, including his last name in his stage name would just be too confusing. I said George Lopez isn't confusing anyone. And Jonah Ray made animal noises. So, the crowd would laugh...and they did. I wanna beat him...beat...beat...

So, all white Europeans, leave! Now! Black & Asian folks can stay if they want, as long as they know this is our land. But we can't be this uncompromising. Because we're part of them and part of you all. We're Native, White, Black, and even Asian 24,000 years ago! So, beat back against the green light...all the way to the motherland if you got to...

124

Putting any labels on us, and putting us in a box and putting that box wherever's most comfortable for you is all…is that all that matters most?

So, keep all your empathy. Keep all your search for our beating pulse! Keep posting Che Guevara and Frida Kahlo. Even though they would've beat and shunned your asses for being such performative rebels for social trophies while smiling at yourselves in the mirror. Two beats? No beats?

We'll get haircuts from Ruben from East LA, "Yeah, mang! They gotta call you Professor mang! You gonna get all the women with the blue eyes and the big asses essay!" I wanted to beat Rubin for being so stereotypical. I wanted to find that beat…in our wrists and in our necks…

Sayin' it like Magneto, "you are right to fear us. We are the future. We are the ones who will inherit this earth!" That helps no one, except white chicks who wanna fuck so they can feel less racist!

We oughta get our asses beat… for being so shameless. But we'll talk about that after everyone's skin color evolves into a dull, Brazilian beige in about 100 years. Why…are we…having such difficulty finding the beats in our wrists…our necks…our…? We're difficult.

But we'd rather jump from the boat, than be enslaved? What say ye Natives? Die? Be a slave? Be a slaver? We can be all of the above. But to be erased…like never having had beats…

No beats Roberto Clemente…no beats Coco…No beats Hugo Chavez… no beats…No beats…

No beats.

ONE EYE.
Sir-Reyna Lucio

Odin gouged out his own eye to gain wisdom. He *understood* that it's not what or who we gain.

It's all we *lose*. *Loss* gives us perspective. With that, we give a standing ovation to the ones who doll themselves up like punk-rapper-preps.

Purposely acting like bohemian vagabonds, spouting out their political defense for the poor, the deeply oppressed, the unseen disabled! These allies are like All-father, the great whiter god *before* the Neo Abrahamic white God took over. These gods *sacrifice* their power, to be an example of *selfless* choice.

They show us, that there's no price too great to know...as an unknowing, like Socrates. This is the contemporary version of *choosing* to lose an eye, to gain deeper *flavors* of insights. Except, *life* should be the one gouging our eye out. If we *choose* to gouge willingly, just to gain more? That's just some self-centered fake bullshit. A performance, to look and sound *deep* in front of more controlled children of slaves & slaves of children.

Here's more *real* self-sacrifice. We played board games and Uno, with our severely, profoundly disabled sibling. We took turns, buying property for them in Monopoly, playing their draw 4-Uno-cards. But we *never* rolled the dice for them, we never *physically* put the card on the pile for them. Our sibling...did that. Do you know how *odd* it is, to play someone's turn in a game? In life? Especially, when they're supposed to be playing *against* you, your family? Your friends?

When you play that enemy's turn *for* your enemy family, your enemy friends?

Contemporary folks...talk a *big* inclusion game. Have they ever had to walk, into a game of Cards Against Humanity, or some Civilization-building crowd-funding game, or some science-based trivia game, and have to keep their *mouths* shut? *We* keep our mouths shut. Because we don't want to *ruin* their big-dirty laugh, and their brain-stroking ego trip. We don't want to let them know that deep down...We're not having a greater time...

Because there's an empty chair at every game table we've ever sat at. There is a *person* that we're supposed to play for. When we play that way, the entire concept of winning and losing is irrelevant. The idea of individual choice is thrown *deeper* into grey. The *broader* visions of what makes us happy is thrown into...silence. So that everyone else doesn't have to care about who's not in that empty chair. We lose an eye, when we look at the empty seat at *every* table we sit at.

We keep *silent* about our lost eye. To let smarter, happier, more competitive people, *exude* confidence. About the people they *think* they're including. We don't rain on them, unless they *dare* us. But with all their vision, they *rarely* notice that we have one eye. And even if they *do* notice, they *never* understand, that it was NOT *us* who gouged out our eye... It was life. Life is always sitting at the table with us.

We're *obsessed* with shitting on Cis white boy from the burbs, sitting in the wrong seat. Get the fuck up!

Life plays a turn for someone who is there *solely* to be with us. And not because of the type of game we're playing. Odin sacrificed his eye to gain wisdom. But he never attained it. And now we know why. That's why I've *purposely* lost almost every competitive game I've *ever* been a part of.

I'm playing for someone, who's not there with us. Someone, I see sitting in that empty chair. I'm playing with one eye, tied behind someone else's back. We've got *more* real life to deal with.

One eye tied behind someone else. One eye...tied behind...One eye.

STATUE
Elaine Nadal

My lover said he wanted to eat my face.
He was smitten, entranced by its roundness
and the sleepy eyes adorning it, which, according to him,
had the power to make anyone go mad with curiosity
of the weight in its sail.

I'm his muse presiding over shores.
He's a passionate man, noticing every detail.
He appreciates how— in a pensive state— I tap my chin
with my index finger or the way my nose flares
when I'm provoked.

He holds me tightly, and although he's incapable of hurting a fly,
I can't help crossing the skyline of imagination and bewilderment.

I find myself in new form, not in a painting covered in geometric shapes
or draped in silk and linen, but in a garden. I'm made of marble. My body
is less proportionate than what I thought. There, after the long pathway of
    stones,
I stand coquettishly next to the honey locust tree with four tulips in my hands
and the right side of my face missing.

My Grandmother's Chest
Skylar J Wynter

My grandmother's chest, which I inherited at her bequest,
has two grown men struggling to bear the weight of it.
And, as they place it haphazardly down in the space
I have made for it,
I know it is full to the brim of all the things
that will trigger a journey into childhood memory.
I know, before I lift the solid wood lid
carved with intricate designs that tell their own story,
the things within are all that remain of a life lived.
When I peek inside, her possessions remind me of holidays spent
sleeping on a mattress on the floor at the end of her bed,
feeling loved and content.
The sight of her knitting needles conjure
the click clacking song that could be heard all year long
as she knitted and purled wisdom subliminally
into legwarmers and jumpers for me.
I can picture the hot afternoons spent inside with the curtains drawn
as I hold a small cardboard box with its corners torn
containing two tiny decks of cards, one pink one blue
that she would use to teach me patience.
And I wonder if these are the things
she wanted to leave me with.
Did she really want me to have her treasured game of Scrabble,
kept immaculate in its box to remind me of
the incredible vocabulary she passed on by placing letters on a board?
When instead, she could have shared it sharing the words
she kept trapped behind a ribcage that should have snapped
under the weight of all the horrors unsaid and packed back
at the back of her throat that surely ached with the constraint of
their containment.
She went to her death, chest heavy.
Leaving me a heavy chest of things
that tell me nothing of the life she lived.
She went to her death, chest heavy.
Leaving me without the most important thing.

129

Her story.
She went to her death, chest heavy,
and I now have a heavy chest of memories
That are only my side of her part in my story
And I am sorry,
now I know what she boxed up inside her body,
that I could never unpack her chest
the way I am unpacking this one.
Taking each item with reverence and gentleness.
Examining, validating and rehoming it
so eventually there would be an empty space
of weightlessness.
An empty space to make breathing space
in a chest that must have always felt breathless
under the weight of violations inflicted upon it.
An empty space to make heart space
that would have opened her up to receiving the love
directed her way but she could never trust.
An empty space that even if filled with nothing
would have been better weightless than weighted
with the unspoken trauma of misuse and abuse
she had to deal with.
An empty space that would have meant she had gifted me
her story to store alongside the memories
I am unpacking from her beautiful wooden chest.
That I inherited, at her bequest.

I WILL LEAVE QUIETLY
Reese North

lay my body down
on this warm and mysterious earth

look up at the clouds
and watch them pass

smell the rich humus of a thousand years
and listen to the songs of evening birds

draw in my final breath
and let go of all that held me here

I will leave quietly

How to Catch a Body
Shawn Renee

I hear him
tell her
this will be a casual
thing.
Watch him
check her for
loose strings
and webbed feelings
he could get
caught in.
Then I watch as he
touches her,
and the smile
that cuts into her
cheeks
as she purposefully
forgets
to tell him
her skin is made
of quicksand
and he will never
be able to
pull himself
out of her again.

IF I WERE TO MEET YOU
Tim Evans

If I were to meet you
Down by the harbour wall
As the shadows start to lengthen
And the seagulls wheel and call

Where the waves cry to the shoreline
And the sunlight dazzles the sea
And I have no expectations
Of a truth to set me free

And if we started out
Just from that time and space
With disbelief and doubt
Banished from the place

Would you come with me upon the ship
That sails upon this tide
Across futures quite untested
And oceans yet untried

And risk it all on the throw of a dice
Where luck is all laid down
Beneath the cobblestones, the beach
And the rocks of the lost and found

And would you voyage with me
To the valleys of the sun
Be my lover, my companion
Until all the days are done

And the present and the past collide
And the shape the spirits take
Are only promises cast like bread
On the belly of the lake.

ON BREATHING
Nina Adel

I felt my
father's last breath, my
hands
on his chest –
the right side –
as he had felt my
first –
my right side, what was
Me.

relief whipped through me,
and shame.

was that what
he felt about
mine?

or did he
miss
my first breath?

what was my breath
to him,
anyway?

Boone and Crockett
JR Robles

November leaves
fell like vacuum
bodies. Direct. No
flitting dead
in dead space.
I donned
the closest I
had to hunting
gear: denim
jacket jogging pants
dull gas station
pocket knife
red gloves pair
of old Reeboks
and set
upon the trail
to Pawpaw's singlewide
out past
parents' chicken farm
where I lived
a boy.

Hunting squirrel
I found rigorous
like pointillism chess
or baking
I followed squat
legs the rifle
sticking out
as tattered denim
can in deep
Tennessee hollers.

Pawpaw
says squirrel season
never ends on
our land.

He waved
fingers at eyes
pointed circles signaling
Stop. Wait.
No beaten paths.
After, he asked
What happens
next time when
I'm gone dead
you're stalking
solo these woods
lose your
bearings? Can you
place your way
back home?

I recall
how the universe
shifted on firing
and reconstituted
in the smoke
powder dust
suspended stamp read
dead dead dead
your early dinner
is dead.

After skinning
dressing and fileting
our prey singing
muses seasoning
castiron browning first
dropping flesh marinated
remnants simmering,
Pawpaw says songs
were written when
we waited
salivary for secrets.

Dipping in
pone rising gilded
glinting in windowlight
Vapors carried
scent time arrowheads
land and property
pursuits, fruits
pats on backs
attaboys never said
tasting memory
I never knew
it would be
so permanent.

COLLAPSING STARS
Jo Collins

I wasn't always small
I grew into it
The way magnolia blossoms learn to snap shut in December
The way we learn to be weightless in space

This purgatory felt like floating and I wanted to stay
To turn my bones inside out, waiting for the light
In forever-expanding places where bodies are nothing but celestial

Me@me
Do you love me?
Here, yes.
On a silent dance floor in the Earth's sky
Where mirrors tell no fictions
And the other shoe never drops

Where dark matter collapses
To become small again

DREAMING IN REPOSE
Shawn Renee

I cleansed my casket today,
pristine as a puddle
and sparkling like dander
caught
at the crisp edges of the sun.
My death - made perfect
in defect.
A little to the left of the
moon in full bloom.
Just out of night-sight
(or the public's view).
Feet planted but infertile.
Mind in thirst
but over watered.
Soaked
through sodden bone and
limp skin,
like root rot in debugged soil.

Unkempt
and unkept,
though I stick like seedlings
to everything
that will only rub me away,
in shadow
and in shame.
But as long
as my casket is clean
my death
will be beautiful.

BLACK BODY
MAMA .

if a black body falls and there are no cameras around to record it, does it
    still make a sound?
does it sound heavy like rocks in it sinking to the bottom of the river?
or does it sound hollow like tree trunks of the branches it hangs from

does its scream reach the ears of its ancestors?
u hear the wind breaking
ships shaking
shape shifting
veil lifting

tell me, does it sound like "kah kah"
they switched out white hoods for blue badges
the hood can't breathe and it's tragic
death used to look like the middle passage
now it's in a life sentence given out to the masses
my nigga g. lock got jammed up for a gun that wasn't even his
that's 25 to life bruh who tf gone take care of his kids

viewing his life through a window
smoking indo for my kinfolk
put one in the air; fuck 12
i'm a stoner bitch i want all the smoke
blow the apple out watch a pig choke
asphyxiation by uniformed knee
it seem to be, time for a revolution
nah fuck allat it's time for a riot
all black with the ski mask
top back and we ridin
my team we comin heavy
with trash bags, know they hefty
blacked out for when we max out
tinted windows in the chevy

i write this letter in the spilt blood of my brothers and sisters
now u shut up and listen
we demand our 40 acres and a mule
niggas prolly sell em for a chain but that don't make no difference

tired of being patient
we been sleeping long enough
still tryna wake up from the bedtime stories y'all read to us
from genesis to revelations got our minds in cuff
got us giving away our power and wondering why life so tough
it's
pastors out here paying past stars to pray in the pulpit
shepherd preying on his flock for a cool fit
how he look so clean in his suit on sunday morning,
he wash his money in tithes and offerings
drug game kinda important

he ain't no prophet
just a crook in expensive shoes yelling "won't he do it" for profit

y'all got us preferring light skin and a big ass
on the auction block i mean instagram for some quick cash
just to go spend it on a new bag
whole lotta ass and no assets; that's so sad
we gotta get rid of that mentality
saying we "chasing a bag" but in reality
we still slaves
say u free
but i bet that money tell u how to behave

it's still magick in our blood
cut me and i bleed miracles
black women are spiritual

black women be home, be holy, be heavenly
black women be church
not church's
black women be more than breasts and thighs
black WOMB-MAN be her name
so say it
say her name say her muhfuckin name
if no one was around u
would u confess
that we're blessed
and u get down for the brown too
would u admit that our culture surrounds u
how u once were lost but a black woman found u
that was me btw
the one popping her gum and beating her head
the one who ain't tryna hear nun a broke nigga said
the one that work these streets and prolly been in yo senators bed
the one that get a i love u text and leave em on read

it's been a mississippi minute since this country sent me one of them
liar liar pants on fire u just burning hem
negro spirituals to get us through the day churching hymn
this country is in shambles cause it run by hims

black woman be mother, be nature

black woman be magician
cut her rage in half and make it disappear into a black hat for men to
    adorn themselves in

black women be arsonists
and burn this country to the ground

How To Write About Black People
Tiana Clark

for white people[1]

Here's how you write about Black people.
You don't—

                Start with my body

or their bodies

                You start

with your own,   with the gaze:

white hands   reaching

for your own   knots

loosening   (the constricting)

construct   of race

with gratitude   and delight.

It doesn't have to start with straining.
It doesn't always have to be about the aboutness
of difference. Start with laughter. Start with your mother
or your breakfast. What did you put in your coffee?
If you take it black, then it's okay to make a joke of it here.
We need a release valve too. Don't apologize. Just keep buying
our books. And not just the ones about pain. I mean buy
those too, but there are also other books by Black authors
about joy and pleasure and time travel that you should
check out. And keep listening. And keep showing up.
And keep asking better questions about yourself
to yourself. You've got this. I know you do. I love you.

[1]This poem is also dedicated to that one white guy in workshop who asked me not to speak
if I didn't like his poem about race. Did you ever rewrite that poem? Are you okay? It seems
no one has heard from you. I love you, too.

HATRED
KHAOS

I've always hated white folk
Though for the love of God
I don't know why

Perhaps it's because I'm from Mississippi
And I've watched too many of my people at their hands die

I remember
Emmett Till
The way his brutal torture and murder
Made his mother cry

I remember
The scottsboro boys
Nine lives
Ruined by some white girl's lie

Not to mention
Burning crosses
Run off livestock
Shot cattle
Barns full of grain set on fire
Plus roasted horses

Perhaps my people in the past did not hate as much
Still their fear made them lost to us

I hate the white doctors
Not just because of AIDS
Remember Tuskegee
Forty years of untreated syphilis
What did that cost us
Forced sterilization
Whole generations not born
So how can we as a people
Even begin to mourn

Perhaps I'm just old and paranoid
With all our men off to war
Shot down by them and
Police in our streets
And
One another

Prisons filled to the brim
With
Father
Son
Husband in law
And
Brother

Who is left to fill the void
Our women
Women without men

Left to burden our fear
And
Their sin

Tempted always by a bigger house
A faster computer mouse
Men with money enough to be considered a spouse

Sooner, not later
Forced to give in to someone with a evil grin

See how cold the white
Man's law
Flooding our neighborhoods with arms
And
Snow already ready
While not allowing their hatred of my people to ever thaw

145

Still
Some ask me
What I hate
them for

I've seen people fired Christmas week
With children at home
Fired regardless of how well they perform
Fired by people whose hearts have turned to stone
People's whose hatred tells them
Black people don't belong

I hate them not because I believe
I am right
And
They are wrong

I hate them because they dance not to the rhythm of life
They seem to have in their hearts
No love
No song
They seem to vent their hatred and fears
Against any people that seem physically or morally strong

Then again
Inside myself
Just for having this
Hatred
I could possibly be
Wrong
Shalom

MY DREAM
KHAOS

It's as if in my dream
Such a frightening dream
I lay face down
On filthy pavement
In the rain

Arms stretched behind me
Causing arthritic shoulder sockets to radiate unbearable
Pain

Knee weighing hard
On an already once broken neck
That feeling
Of
Life leaving
Just as it had come
Stressed
Full of fright
Painfully uncomfortable
And
Wet

Evil was smiling down at me
Face showing a hateful
disdain
disgust
Almost a sexually charged
Bloodlust
There for all the world to see

Sensing my demise
I cried out of tear filled eyes

MOMMA

MOMMA

We'll meet again
Graveside

There'll be no waiting
On a third day
For my spirit to rise

While the righteous world fights back shock and tears

The unrighteous worry about
Property
Loss of revenue
All the while
Their losing privilege
Being the greatest of their fears

Why was Martin's dream so much different from mine
He traveled to the mountaintop

Looked over

And yet

He could not see that the bigotry of supremacy
Would still reign
And Satan's disciple would have a hold on morality and justice

Lo

Over all these fifty some years of time

IF YOU RUN INTO SOMEONE YOU HAVEN'T SEEN IN 7 YEARS, YOU DON'T HAVE TO SAY HI
Nick Bush

The cells composing the old them—gone,
a batter of ether migrating back to the universe
the new you doesn't owe the old you a courtesy conversation,
a grope of common ground when common ground has
slid like tectonic plates, a push of time-space continuum
that has brought you both to this moment, this place,
this crossroads of old consternations and new resolutions.

Many Marches and many more moons
from that time when you were neighbors
or lovers have come and gone. Hopes wilted and blossomed,
new hopes grown and moving, balanced like funambulists,
with the gravity of new challenges
and the light air of new visions,
that unclench the past and reach, finger-splayed, towards the future.

THE BABY MEETS HER BODY FOR THE FIRST TIME
Fizza Abbas

A cloak, as layered as a sky, meets a fine, delicate ballerina in
salmon-pink ballet shoes. The half-knit shadow, the sugar-plum fairy
twirling in warm white light.

The meeting takes place between the two in the baby room at the Holy
Family Hospital. I eavesdrop and hear lifestyle tips exchanged in quiet.

This dark, ghastly guardian speaks to the baby in a low, hushed voice,
with baby showing her focus with a yawning chasm.

Tip number one: eat air with a grain of sand for I like to retrace footsteps.
Tip number two: drink a hot, simmering pot of vapourous juice as I like to
see my veins popping out during the rain.

Tip three: start with soft rompers, rock the hip and trendy and sigh with
woollen open backs as I like to believe I have eclectic tastes. Don't yell,
cry like the ocean waves hitting the shore.

But loudly. Just mark your presence. I know you are currently in
economic crisis for definitions and words. Let me share the basics: Air is a
hard-hitting slap of the wind, rain is a nature's pat.

Waves are relentless curves in motion. That's it for today. I shall meet you
more often now that you're with me. In me, Ha-ha. Let's doze off now.

I watched the two drifting off. It was quite late. When I looked at my
watch, it was 52,5600 days and 3,15,36000 seconds.

TO THE MEN IN MY LIFE.
Kimberly Jay aka Special K

I am not a cow
Yet you continue to give me your regurgitated lies,
Again and again,
Forcing me to digest them
But instead of passing them through a four stomach system,
They pass through my soul
And are birthed into the lives of my children.
But I am not a cow, so you won't call it cud.
You will call it love.

And I, whose birth was covered in a mixture of the ancestors' blood and
man's knotted up rough cord
Have become the seed that encourages the grass to grow…
But blow after blow and lie after lie–
I have been trampled on.
Now I am no longer fertile ground and have become the tree
And your strands that flow inside of me have manifested into rope–
Where you swing:
Your body mimicking the folly and fun you promised me this life would
bring.

This is the story they will tell.
They will not remember how I was pulled, shaped and molded from your rib.
Nor how I sat majestically beside you–
A mighty force to be reckoned with.
You'll not hear them say a thing about how
It was you and I that saved the day, with our very own melanin,
Pulling light into their dark ages.

I am not a cow, but they will display my body for all to see,
Repeatedly,
Until you forget the dynamics that was you and me.

They will tear us apart
And where I once was connected,
The protector of your heart–
They will perform surgery and remove all traces of what was once there:
Me.
And you will let them.
You will believe it when they say I didn't want you
That I saw no value or worth within your human shell.
Thus, the birthing of lies will begin.

They will beat you into submission.
They will breed you until that is all you think you've ever been.
And if you dare to show an ounce of the strength that was once there–
They will teach you how to round up your kin;
Pin them in and brand them too.
You will not know the depths of which that ink you use sets in.

I am not a cow; my skin won't regenerate.
My neck will be covered in the shards of your wire
And my tears will be the sweat which pours from me as you perspire.

I am not a cow, but they will instill in you
That I am a commodity, my body nothing more than
A replaceable source for your energy.
They will not tell you that it is I,
Who can stir up everything within your soul, including life itself;
Or that I am the helpmate to all your goals.

I am not a cow.
But they will tell you this is the life cycle
And the only way for you to win.
They will tell you that THIS is how you become a man.

They will hand you the gun.
I will not run.
I will look at you with sadness and hurt pouring from my eyes.
I will beg you to remember…
I am not a cow.
You will pull the trigger, anyhow…
And when the same blood that was present at my birth
Spills over you and your streets–
They will tell you that your sin is not on their hands
And lay me at your feet.
They will lock you away in a metal land
And the city will throw away the key.
And no one will stand for you on that great day of judgement.
No one, that is, except for me- the woman you once knew.

The only way to make what they say untrue
Is to wake up and see that
I am not a cow,
But a woman beside you
And we, a King and a Queen are more than just royalty.
We are the birth, legacy and continuation of the black family
And because of this–
We must succeed.

ORIGEN
Leslie Shakira Garcia

you must find your womanhood on the dance floor
when people say you look good tonight wink as if to
say I look good every night but thank you for
noticing
take your tequila shots
like you rotate salsa partners
once an hour
let washing machine hips stir ancestry
listen to the conga
skin on wood
drum beating pulse into
memories of African slaves
who hid their gods in song
and danced
despite the tobacco plantations
bending them backwards
beads of sweat hung familiar
to the smalls of their backs
West Africa and Spain met
on the dusty dance floor of the Caribbean
to birth Salsa
which conceives You
a century later in the clubs of Brooklyn
where your parents are not yet
your parents but instruments
trombone thighs keeping tempo with clave arms
spinning to the bar and
ordering another round of shots
like you will
21 years and nine months later
on your birthday

ADONI
Mel Bradley

You sent your angel, your messenger
To tell me I must be
Mother
I bore that
For you
For all the world
I carried him
Kept him
Guarded him
Watched him enter this world
Air filling his lungs
In first shocked breath
Comforted him
Suckled him
Watched him grow

With the understanding that this world
would hold great expectations for him
Witnessed him reach manhood
through uncertainty
Fleeing from persecution
And death
As a babe
Wrapped in my arms

I watched him grow

Question those around him
In your name
Follow paths I didn't understand
Surround himself with difficulty
Crowds that gathered to hear
Him speak your words

Where are they now?

155

Is this what you wanted from me?
Bring a child into this world
And watch him die
Be tortured
Tried as a criminal
Held accountable for giving people hope
And now,
Endure further
As he is
Murdered
Unable to intervene
Because this, is your plan

I kept him safe all those years
How am I supposed to let it happen?
What kind of mother
Does that make me?

Adoni
Tell me
How?

DEAREST WOMEN
Mel Bradley

Fragility only in eggshell prison confines
Fabricated from the fallacy of men
Father on high, inspiring words and deeds
Atrocities that perpetuate the shame you carry
In my name

Removed me from your likeness
Stripped me from my womanly nature
To hold you in this guise, unnatural
Strictures formed to keep you
Tethered in insecurity

Humility, obedience
Simplicity of manner
Purity, unimpeachable
Causing no end of pain
Whispered in your ears
From you were but a babe

Daughters, taught from crib
To womanhood to fear themselves
and each other
Born as vessel, to be broken
Reassembled in misshapen form
Chattel, ownership never your own

Barefooted, I am made to stand
On serpent's head
To teach you that I conquered
That which you will never
Show you, your deficiencies
As role model, out of reach

You carry blame in your bodies
Sorrow, a river, born in your veins
Concealment of sex, ensure its protection
Kept sacred
Given when conquered, worthy champion
Found
You carry the fault of female nature

Our likeness only in purposeful motherhood
Creator, engineer, nurturing bodyguard
Biology punished
As you beg for forgiveness
In fulfillment of your designated role
Purified through prayers of onlookers

You have wept for your sisters taken
Made to walk in penance for crimes
Against their prescribed virtue
Babies torn from their arms
And sold or malnourished
Discarded in disgrace

They've depicted me in acceptance
To show you
How to hold submission in your gaze
Tranquility and sweetness of heart
Endurance through trials
Suffering your legacy

My tears are for you
Stolen
My heart pierced and wounded
In watchful repose
Helpless I carry the weight of you
Complicit in the thrashing of
Female flesh
And severed spirit

Now, I watch you rise
Slowly awakening from this
Haze of deception
Meet each other in sisterly adoration
Journey together towards emancipation
Reparation for generations soaked in hurt
Healers
Warriors
Women.

REFLECTION
Dominique "Substance" Hayes

Look at you
Traveled realms just to manifest in this world
Diamond in the rough
Fresh like spring water
Glistening pearl
Underappreciated
Image dismantled
devalued
Do they know who you are?
Goddess
God-is
God is
Her reflection
Introspected
Wombs of crucifixion
Laced with healing
Royal aura
Clothed in white
Priestess of Night
Healer of Day
Look at you
Overcoming the world

CHEE INSIDE ME
Gary Huskisson

The chee is me
Spiritually mindfully
Depression is drip fed inside me
Drag into the world lyrically

Soul a foetus in a land where I am alien
Shadows of joy diverted to the colon
Letters to my Father are inspirations
Chee, never stops with Amen,
Spirit wants to go again and again.

There is always a trauma behind a smile,
Always smile in front of a trial,
Chee nurtures the holy ghost,
With blessings that blossom that are fertile

I am stillborn, my eyelids rest in peace,
With my brows spread, with no breeze,
My nostrils become aroused,
By the aroma of intoxicating incense,
Igniting the ceremonial vibe

The serpent tongue rises through the mist
Cleansing the air with saliva,
Catalyst for drips to become resonance

Grasping a sparrow's tail through the haze
Ward off left, P'eng
Ward off right
Roll back, Lu
Squeeze, Chee,
Warding of the toxic demons,
Racism, sexism, and global poverty

Chee circulates,
Churning up the intestines
Radiating the cheeks

A single whip, breaks the storm in the chee,
Stork cools its wings,
Generating backbone
Cleansing, eradicating hate
Say it louder, be kinder

The mind plays the Pi pi
Quaves burst out of the integers,
Rotating my palms,
Like Saturn rings stroking the heart

Time to wave hands in clouds,
Parting wild horse's mane,
Treating the spleen, repulsing the monkey
Returning the tiger from where it came

A moment silence,
The serpent tongue creeps down,
Forgiven
A fair lady levitates above
She takes my hand till I come to a pause,
Vertical eyes open,
Spirit no longer stillborn, fearless

LEASE
Ross Donlon

"And summer's lease hath all too short a date" ~ William Shakespeare

It's not as if there were documents signed
when I took possession. The understanding
between owner and me had to be open,
since both knew my dwelling would change.
     I've had no real complaints.
The foundations always had a yen to shift
and my preference for a lighthouse topped
with a view of the past, present and future
only got so far as rickety stairs to an attic,
two bay windows looking straight ahead.

Of course, it would be difficult for any tenant
to maintain the space as first occupied. To ask:
Nothing on the walls. No extensions is fanciful
and especially hard to comply with the latter,
since extensions happen of their own accord.

And how to complain to the eternal landlord
regarding any structural deterioration, notably
in private places, the bathroom, the bedroom,
since despite the wear of passing years,
wiring and plumbing remain: *Original. As supplied.*

I accept that the lease is binding
and, as it's a handshake deal,
my infant paw clasping the finger of God,
I respect the undertaking will only last
until one of us dies.

UNEVEN THINGS
Katie Thompson

My ears are uneven
and I found out everyone's
ears are uneven!
So I'm strangely different
but strangely the same perhaps.
Facts known
or anomalies needed,
It is a toss up.

What else is uneven
Uneven roads
Uneven pavement.
I'm racking my brains
Or is it I am racking my BRAIN?
Well, my brains are probably uneven
as well, probably
from my uneven ears, so
thanks for that ears.

Society is uneven,
privilege is uneven
people magnify it,
even if they don't mean to.
Opinions make us uneven,
but do they have to?
Any unfairness seems uneven,
right now me and my daughter
are uneven, because I tower
over her, but that may change soon
and she will be the winner in the
uneven contest with her mom.

Growing up,
my brothers and sister
were uneven in treatment and
pecking order, but we
were very even when we were
corporally punished.
Sometimes it's a bit
uneven when bad things happen to
good people, and it seems to
always be that way.

It was uneven that one day you
loved me no more,
because we started out even,
and continued even,
and then became uneven
when you decided it was so.
So still I feel a bit uneven, and a bit
unhinged at times, but here we are
even and uneven over here trying not to be.

1
Zach Nicholson

Did you know I've never slept next to someone so stone still
Like death
Not the metaphor type
But the cold cadaver kind
And you might have been dead then, I thought,
But you choked on your own spit half an hour ago
And I worried so much that you would wake up
Before your body could purge the poison from your brain
Before your body could remember who you were supposed to be

Did you know I never knew a person could be split in two
And still go on living
As if a tiny shadow throttled you
Leaving pale ghost fingerprints around your neck
Hardly there at all, so we don't have to talk about it
Until the intruder night makes you complete darkness,
And we talk about it then, sure,
But the night falls away with the morning light as the icy green of your
eyes adjusts to the new day

Did you know it doesn't fall away for everyone, though,
Because I was there all night with your other half
And it was just me and you—the one who looks like you, anyway—
And I will never forget that face
So exact in your likeness
But something broken, gnashing like hounds to escape,
Spit flying from your mouth,
Whiskey leaping from your breath

I hold tight to this thing that looks like you
And I lie to it
And I say, I love you, I love you
Go to sleep, go to sleep
And I hope to god the lullaby works
So I can wake up in the morning when your darkness lies dormant
And try so hard to forget the night that you'll never remember

WALKING EARLY
Walker Bass

God said don't sleep in
Said, once man gets comfortable
he sacrifices
less
Said, remember that rich white church?
Emptiness is to be sought for
unless it's hollow
Said, get up before the dogs bark,
and the deer, fleeting, are just silhouettes
Said, footsteps are a prayer
Said, get up early
and let the tattoo
of yours
thrum

VIGIL FOR THE CHRISTCHURCH MOSQUES
Tim Evans

During Friday prayers on 15 March 2019, a white supremacist, part of the so-called 'alt-right,' opened fire with semiautomatic weapons at the Al Noor mosque and at the Linwood Islamic Centre in Christchurch, New Zealand. He killed 51 people and wounded 40. In many towns, including Swansea, South Wales, vigils were organised in solidarity with our Muslim brothers and sisters under attack.

A rainy evening, thick with cloud,
The best part of the day long past,
I stood, part of a silent crowd,
As the ghosts of the dead went drifting past.

We have to reach for the human heart,
The human touch, the human mind
When demons hop and lives are smashed
And love is broken, deaf and blind.

So we stood on the pavement, slick with rain,
And our voices reached out to the stars,
And we reached out to each other's pain
Like an old song played on an old guitar.

But love alone is not enough
On a night so full of human hurt,
And peace won't come if the price of peace
Are bodies broken in the dirt.

'Never again', we used to say.
Well, 'never again' is coming fast.
We stand united – we stand as one,
Against these monsters from the past.

We stand as one – we stand together
In power, hope and unity.
Strike my brother, strike my sister
And you strike me.

I.M. EMMA (15 YEARS YOUNG)
Reese North

A child's dream
cast within a world of storms -This life.
A sudden influx of light that crafts
a myriad of forms.

A thousand dramas create a mosaic
to hold a generation entranced
by fate's
                    mirror
                    in the air.

Thunder's drum rolls in hills
while woodwind trees blow a dirge
to passing life   and memories.
          A glimmer of renewal remains
          after earth   cremates   her own.

THE HEART IS A PLACE
Kat Marsh

The heart is a place one turns inward to embrace.

Sometimes our fears and impatient minds
Leave what's needed to stay hidden and blind.

The mind can be a river guiding you there.
The mind can be a storm thrashing your care.

The heart will keep beating in dedication, through contemplation.

The heart is a place not designated by lands
Or, only those creatures who call themselves man.
The heart is a place of open hands.

The heart is a place which is always nigh
Whether the body is far or by one's side.

The heart is a place moving in tune
Creating memories upon ocean runes.

The heart is a place that rests upon medaled and free fingers
That feels the call of love's linger.

The heart is a place forged in ice and fire
That has known pain but still aims higher.

The heart is a place I rest my soul
When challenges try to take their toll.
The heart is a place where I rise.

THE TREE THAT HUGGED ITS HUMANS
Bryan Franco

The first house my parents bought
11 Burton Drive in Atlanta, Georgia
was a split-level brick house
with a magnolia tree in the front yard.
The first and only house my parents built
305 Fern Hill Court in Mobile, Alabama
was a larger split-level brick house,
oaks and pines dotting the backyard.
As a surprise for mom, dad had a juvenile magnolia
planted in the front yard.
Reita Ann Paplanus Franco a.k.a. Mommy Salami
was awed by magnolia blossoms.
Unbeknownst to her husband a.k.a. Goode,
this tree was male, which didn't bloom,
but it grew tall with twisted, gnarled branches,
leaves as large as my adult hands,
rich forest green: crisp, slick, shiny
with a velvety soft underside.
As beautiful and aromatic blossoms of magnolias are,
the leaves give them their iconic strength of character.

My mother's tree is now 41 years old:
tall and wide as a New England town square Christmas tree.
When mom moved to a patio home in 1993,
it was half its current size.
I believe pieces of my family's souls live in the tree.
The roots are my father digging deeper in the ground yearly, providing
    stability ----
season after season, milestone after milestone, hurricane after hurricane,
barbecue after barbecue.
The branches are my brothers and myself: the longer they grew,
the more offshoots they produced, the more life we lived:
crushes, first dates, bar mitzvahs, graduations, college, adulthood.
Mom is the leaves soaking in sunlight nourishing her tree with unbridled love:
absorbing ever-present rainstorms that plague Mobile, Alabama

and turmoil that beset our family.
Reita, or Atier, as Goode called her, was a force to be reckoned with
and was never without a hug for anyone in her family.

After mom died,
I flew into Mobile from Maine.
I asked my brother Paul to drive by the house.
The tree was magnanimous.
Paul stopped the car for a minute;
We stared at a chunk of our history
then left for the funeral home to view the body.
I knew if I walked over to the tree and touched a leaf,
I would have been touched by my mother's soul,
a soul that would find it impossible
to not hug her son from the afterlife.

BEAT
Joshua Parrish

After 3,000 miles cross country
Brain and body beat
To calm my nerves
Beat my liver with liquor
Beat my lungs with smoke
Beat back and forth in bed
The persistent interstate beat
Pervasive in body and brain
My brother and I driving across
America, patrolling our beat
The rhythm of life beating
From a childhood journey
Family seeking a different beat
My parents beat from life, work
And a prophetic cross country drive
Now I am older and think
Of my bare feet as they beat
Across high school graduation stage
Of how my brother's fists
Beat my head, bouncing off the floor
How I beat body and brain
Things I would throw away
If only the constant beat
Of dreams would stay

CÀ PHÊ SỮA NÓNG AND FRYBREAD
Chance Chambers

after Papalagui Exposed at OZ Arts Nashville

Rattle my soul against opium-stained tracks,
a Lào Cai to Hanoi railway where specters
of Hmong villagers watch all this comfort pass.

Shake my history at the hinges and turn my taste
for twentieth-century wooden archways
and balconies to marble and metal.

Meet me for cà phê sữa nóng in a bakery
built on shadows of lotus leaves and rice farmers,
where "madame" rolls off a tongue,
butter from a croissant.

Walk with me on streets where I photographed
fruit vendors and cyclo drivers, where I was given
a sacrament of ginger candy that tasted like forgiveness,
where I broke the body of freedom
and left nothing but baguette crumbs.

And if I die before I take
the last flight out of Tân Sơn Nhất,
bury me facing the west. The Hmong say
that's the direction of death.

I'll watch the story of my ancestors flash
against a stolen sky, scenes from a reel packed away
under pox blankets, dusty rifles, and broken treaties,
all the tools that built my world.

I'll smell the oil and dough cooking on the corner
of Edgehill and Villa, where I ate frybread
like a tourist in the city I call home.

I'll breathe the steam of sage and sweet grass
on lava rock in a ceremony that was never mine.

I'll hear again the story of my great grandfather,
how he arrived at his daughter's wedding
on horseback, dressed in the clothes
of a Cherokee chief. A thimble's worth
of my spit says that never happened.

And when I try to tell a new story, but can speak
only of missionaries and bombs, whisper to me
all the pretty names for occupation:

colony, commonwealth, salvation, empire

LISSIMS, NISSIMS, ISSIMS (BODY POLITICS)
James C. Floyd Jr. aka The Jefferson Street Poet

       A.
take children capable of unconditional love and:
1. Open their heads
2. Take their brains
3. Devour them while
    they are warm and
      fresh.
           B.
strike the match that sets young women and men afire and watch with
nods of approval as they:
1. Dance
2. Melt
3. Fade away in
    the agonizing
    flames of what
    you call
    AMBITION!

THE QUESTION OF THE EGG
Amy Hoskins

he took the egg
rubbed it between his hands
until the shell was gone
then i was exposed

maybe i grew around what was left
until the shape of the egg was lost
in folds of my heart tissue

or maybe it drifted in my bloodstream
like a lost craft
a broken plane

did it evaporate in the confusion of the
heat of that summer?
disintegrate
and become part of the invisible
everything where dead leaves and
grandparents go?

unlike you
who can put the tapes on erase
i am haunted by the ghost of a
small unborn bird
wildly shadowing me
pecking, chirping
telling me
maybe it could have flown?

BUT SOME MEN CALL OUT THE RAPISTS
Destiny O. Birdsong

it's true
> you're no swan

and neither
> is this Leda

her dark throat
> gouged

the clot
> of lifeblood

invisible
> against her skin

you're a peacock
> pleading

for his
> nesting hen

(and doesn't
> every woman

need to hear
> at least once

the sound
> of her own keening?)

you nurse
      your cracked

beak
      most beautifully

technicolor
      tears

fanning your back
          as you dip
into
      the goosedown

crowning
         her thighs

you're
    healing her

like a cuckoo
        you build

your nest
      atop

the webbed burn
         on her sternum

you nestle
      your eggs

in the blooming
                bruise of her telling

perhaps
        you're most like

a vulture:
              usually silent

until
        you discover

a curdle
        of maggots

paring
              her perineum

how you
        mourn

what you
              have called

behind
              her back

a carcass

that only
        hours

earlier
      might have been

a feast

for you

     alone

GHOST HOUR, A MONTH AFTER MY MOTHER'S DEATH
Dana Malone

Almost everything can be forgiven

at least
that's what I hoped
across the shatter-proof
partition from a perpetrator

Almost everything rests

on her grave
or the touch of my hand
on her shoulder.
What I did not know
would be the last.

Or her palm between
my shoulder blades
all those childhood nights
I did not think
I could dream

that something besides monsters
would be almost everything.

CROSS-EYED
James C. Floyd Jr. aka The Jefferson Street Poet

Once, as I lay in a meadow
a soft yellow butterfly lit upon the tip of my nose.
And as I observed it closely
the slate-gray clouds changed into horses and teddy bears
and a fluffy castle with windows casting lavender shadows.
The sun became a mouth, opened in silent golden laughter.

And the flowers each played woodwinds
whose music contained a vapor
that transfigured me into a universe
imprisoned inside a dew drop.

Til I fell to the ground and burst
and went shooting into infinity at a thousand light-years per beat.
Past time past substance beyond the end to the beginning
where I find myself
on the tip of the nose
of a dead soldier.

ACKNOWLEDGMENTS

This feels like acknowledging water for giving and sustaining life, but all we have are our words, imbued with our sincerest gratitude.

To Lance Umenhofer, Matt Johnstone, and the team at April Gloaming Publishing: You were the perfect partner to bring this body of poetry to life. No one else could have quite nailed the pulse of our vision—a collection that has global reach, while retaining a distinct Nashville vibration. It was thrilling to have your expert guidance at the helm.

To the Poetry in the Brew founders: Thank you for breathing life into this body. We would not be here today, strong as we are, without your passionate delivery of this community into the world.

To Christine Hall: Because of you, Poetry in the Brew remains sacred space for generosity of spirit, inclusivity, and boundless creative energy. The garden you tend to so sweetly sprouts eternal vegetation.

To Jo Collins: You have this uncanny knack for saying the magic words at the magic moment in a manner that is magical. You are the whole magical package, body-mind-spirit-soul, but instead of getting haughty about it, you hold us up with humor and humility.

To Henry L. Jones: We overflow with thanks for your art, activism, and the powerful truths you speak with compassion. Your creative expressions and the steadfast support you give this community shine beacons of hope and understanding.

To Patrick and our Portland Brew East family: You gave us a home for so many years. We cannot wait until we are reunited again.

To our anthology contributors: We are grateful and elated that you entrusted us with your incredible works of art. Your poetry takes our breath away. These are pieces that must be revisited time and again because they are a force of nature and divine nourishment.

To the publications that bear the torch: "ME/AT" by Ananda Lima originally appeared in *Palette Poetry*. "The baby meets her body for the first time" by Fizza Abbas originally appeared in *Selcouth Station*. Destiny O. Birdsong's "but some men call out the rapists" originally appeared in *Muzzle*.

To our many open mic readers from across the globe: You are the sinew of Poetry in the Brew. You are the muscles and tendon that have kept this body moving forward over the past decade. We hope you'll keep coming back.

CONTRIBUTORS

Fizza Abbas is a writer based in Karachi, Pakistan. Her work has been published in over 70 platforms, both online and in print. Two of her chapbooks are coming out in 2021: *Bakho* (Ethel Zine and Micro Press) and *Ool Jalool* (Fahmidan Publishing). Her goal is to get her work published in 10,000 journals by the end of 2030.

Nina Adel holds an MFA from Hamline University. She's the winner of Bellevue Literary Review 2020 Buckvar Prize for Nonfiction. Published in many literary journals (see list/links at ninaadel.com), Nina teaches at a Nashville-area college, directs the Immigrants Write program and is also a musician. Follow her on Instagram/Twitter @writethinkspeak.

Patricia Alice Albrecht, widely published and beloved by the poetry community, was also cherished for her role in *Jem and the Holograms*, in which she played the antagonist Pizzazz. Her support of fellow poets always proved uplifting, with enduring effects. Amanda Oliver Hendricks shares memories of Patricia, reflecting on the legacy of her work: "On the patio outside of her dining room, Patricia painted sunflowers over the cracks that had formed in the cement. I stepped outside after writing with her one day and found them there growing and thriving—from her heart, to her hand, and to healing what had once been broken. Patricia made beautiful out of brokenness. When I imagine her now, she is holding a bouquet of sunflowers. Her light nourishing them like always. She glowed. Her voice still rises from the words she left behind for us on the page. I can hear her say, 'Write on.'"

Michelle Awad is a Tennessee native who grew up in and around the Nashville area. In 2016, she visited New Orleans for the first time and moved there in 2018 because her soul was homesick for it. She's been a member of the Poetry in the Brew community for the past several years and has enjoyed attending and participating in PitB readings whenever she can, even being a featured poet in June of 2015. In her spare time, you can find her sitting on her back porch in Algiers, sipping a gin cocktail and listening to the sounds of the city. Her dog is probably there, too, protecting the yard from squirrels. For more of her work, you can find her on Instagram: @theconstantpoet.

Walker Bass read at his first Poetry in the Brew in August 2011 and was a frequent reader until his departure from Nashville in 2019. PitB was an important part of his community, and he was enriched every time he attended. Walker now lives in Austin, TX and teaches mindfulness meditation.

Beady Man is a poet, rapper, and activist from Brixton. He has been performing for over a decade on the circuit and is currently working on a solo studio album, along with projects with various bands. He works in the NHS with patients who have complex mental health issues.

Destiny O. Birdsong is a Louisiana-born poet, essayist, and fiction writer whose debut poetry collection, *Negotiations*, was published by Tin House Books in October 2020, and whose debut novel is forthcoming from Grand Central Publishing in 2022. She lives and writes in Nashville, Tennessee.

Mel Bradley is a spoken word artist, writer, playwright/theatremaker, multimedia artist, designer, and actor. A gatherer of the untold stories of women. An outspoken queer feminist performer with a candid voice and an unhealthy obsession with the Virgin Mary. A creative genius with the attention span of a gnat.

Caroline Burrows' latest commission was for Glenside Museum & Bristol Festival of Ideas. She's in *National Flash Fiction Day Anthology*, *Wilfred Owen Journal*, and *Cycle UK Magazine*, has an MA in Creative Writing, teaches, performs, and posts @VerseCycle.

Nick Bush is an associate professor at Motlow State Community College who performs standup comedy and writes poetry and fiction. He is part of a team that manages a Murfreesboro open mic and poetry series. He co-hosts Smokes & Jokes Comedy Show, also in Murfreesboro. His work has appeared in *Mused*, *Literary Yard*, *Baseball Bard*, and *Five-Two Poetry*. Find him on Instagram and Twitter @nickxbush.

Cathy Carson is a cancer nurse, counsellor, and spoken word performer from Northern Ireland. She uses her writing to raise awareness of those who are vulnerable in society. She is published in several anthologies and has performed at festivals and for local radio and television.

Chance Chambers, a former resident of Nashville, now lives in Birmingham, Alabama, with his beautiful wife, Jennifer, and three cats. His work has appeared in *Perfume River Poetry Review*, *Number One: A Literary Journal*, and *Sobotka Literary Magazine*.

Tiana Clark is the author of the poetry collection, *I Can't Talk About the Trees Without the Blood* (University of Pittsburgh Press, 2018), winner of the 2017 Agnes Lynch Starrett Prize, and *Equilibrium* (Bull City Press, 2016), selected by Afaa Michael Weaver for the 2016 Frost Place Chapbook Competition.

Christian J. Collier is a Black Southern writer, arts organizer, and teaching artist who resides in Chattanooga, TN. His works have appeared or are forthcoming in *Hayden's Ferry Review*, *The Michigan Quarterly Review*, *Atlanta Review*, *Grist Journal*, and elsewhere.

Jo Collins (She/Her, Nashville) is a lifetime member of the Brew Crew, thanks to hanging chads and the right words spoken by the right person. On January 12, 2019, Jo performed the world's first erotic poem about Al Gore, after which Christine Hall uttered: "Oh, I hope you'll come back." And, she did.

Michael Collins: "In former lives I worked as a teacher, a nurse, and a community worker. I am currently being supported by the Australian people (pensioner), which leaves me free to participate in personal study, writing poetry and short stories, and engaging in activist activities, which may (but probably won't) get me arrested. A regular at Poetry At The Pub and WordHurl Antislam, as well as several Zoom poetry events, I have (self) published eight CDs and two books of poetry. Looking forward to peace on earth, and goodwill to all."

Carolyn Connolly currently lives in Nashville, TN, where she's a senior at Belmont University with an undergraduate degree in English and a double minor in creative writing and history. She's had work chosen for presentation at the International English Honors Society Convention and has work in, or forthcoming from, *1 Human Journal*, *Allegory Ridge*, and the *Belmont Literary Journal*. When she's not writing about women's lives or working, she's filling out applications for an MFA in poetry with her fingers and toes crossed.

Jeff Cottrill is a fiction writer, journalist, and performance poet based in Toronto. He has headlined in countless literary series across Canada, the U.K., and the U.S. since 2001 and recently finished his seventh or eighth attempt at a first novel.

Andrew P. Dillon earned his BA and MFA from the University of Tennessee. His work is forthcoming or has appeared most recently in *Please See Me*, *Second Chance Lit*, *The Bosphorus Review of Books*, *Analog*, *Stirring*, and Connotation Press. Visit his website at andrewdillonpoetry.com.

Ross Donlon is an Australian poet who has published five books of poems. Winner of two international poetry competitions, he has been featured at poetry festivals both at home and in Europe. His latest collection is *For the Record* (Recent Work Press 2021). www.rossdonlon.com

Ali El-Chaer is a Palestinian-American artist from Nashville, TN. They received their BFA at Austin Peay State University and have featured works in Nashville, Clarksville, and New York. They create a discussion through mixed media processes on the colonization of land, body, mind, and spirit and use intense interpersonal emotions to relate to others. Currently they are expanding their practices into the mutual aid realm by assembling care packages for the houseless and raising funds for folx locally and internationally.

Tim Evans is a poet, writer, and activist. He co-hosts Live Poets, a radical socialist poetry group. His work appears in various journals and anthologies, and in two poetry collections, with a third in preparation. "Most people ignore most poetry because most poetry ignores most people" –Adrian Mitchell.

James C. Floyd Jr. aka The Jefferson Street Poet is a native Nashvillian, educated in its public schools and on its streets of the nineteen fifties and sixties. He is the result of those who tried to kill his spirit when he was lost and those who prayed for him when he couldn't pray for himself. He is a writer.

Bryan Franco lives in Brunswick, Maine. He is a poet and spoken word artist/performer. He was a member of the Portland, Maine, Rhythmic Cypher slam team that competed in the 2014 National Poetry Slam in Oakland, California. He's also a painter, sculptor, gardener, and culinary genius.

Storyteller, part time vegan, and silent ninja, **Craig Freeman** uses writing to find clarity in the human experience.

Erin Gannon is a poet, singer, and biker chick. She holds an MA in Poetry from the Seamus Heaney Centre for Creative Writing at Queens University Belfast and is currently working on her DFA in Creative Writing at the University of Glasgow, where she labors mightily over a long-form poem / rock opera. She co-hosts the Choose Poetry, Choose Life open mic. (choosepoetry.co.uk).

Leslie Shakira Garcia is a Salvadorian-American poet from Brooklyn, New York.

From the edge of Houston, TX, **Angie Marie Gonzalez** is a songwriter and a poet in Nashville. Both through lyrics and spoken word, she crafts a dizzying fever dream that blurs the line between fantasy and personal history, taking the listener on a breathless journey that crisscrosses the country and runs the emotional spectrum. You may have seen one of her poems on the downtown WeGo bus or East Nashville bus shelter in 2019 or heard some of her spoken-word at Poetry in the Brew. Angie hopes to continue expanding her pieces on trauma, hope, and experiences as a queer person of Mexican-American heritage in the South.

Poet **Navita Gunter** writes about struggles, sharing poems about prevailing. Author of *The Day My Vagina Tried to Kill Me* and *N2Words*, Gunter hosted Nashville's first weekly poetry open mic at Kijiji's. The Guthrie, KY-native is a Western Kentucky University graduate who founded the Cervical Cancer Coalition of Tennessee.

Christine Hall was raised in a trailer at the edge of the Adirondacks by troubadours and cultist pornographers. Inculcated with American mythology—tool girl calendars, bible stories, science fiction—she built on this education while hitching across the continent. Now at home in Nashville's arts community, Christine hosts Poetry in the Brew.

Fin Hall comes from and lives in Scotland. He is poet in residence at Aberdeen Folk Club Covideo Sessions, and has work published in various books and papers and online. He has made a short film called *Poets in Therapy*. Fin also produces and hosts the storytelling show *Everybody Has A Story*.

Dominique "Substance" Hayes is a Nashville-based poet and the Founder of Chō·zęn., a self-love brand. Her mission is to illustrate her journey to wholeness and self-actualization. Her poems are clear views of her truth. The poem "Reflection" is an illustration of self-love and the realization of divinity—past, present, and future.

Amanda O. Hendricks is a red-dirt poet recently published in *Wordpeace* and *The Basil O'Flaherty Feminists' Voice*. Hendricks writes words daily on the hearts of her young sons in Birmingham, AL. She feels incredibly blessed to have connected with the Poetry in the Brew family—honored to host, feature, step up to the open mic, and to just listen. For more, please visit anythingbutsilent.wordpress.com.

Hil Hoover writes poetry, flash fiction, love letters to strangers, tabletop character sheets, and clumsy bootprints all over Middle Tennessee. Bios, not so much. They are nonbinary, geeky, and in love with words, trees, and chili chocolate.

Amy Hoskins is a poet and visual artist creating with disabilities from her home in South Nashville, TN. Hoskins has hosted a poetry open mic since June, 2017 and hosts the monthly Gestalt Poetry Open Mic, which is virtual for now. Amy has had eleven poems published in the US, and one in Amsterdam. www.amyhoskins.com

Gary Huskisson is a storyteller specialising in education, therapy, and Jazz Poetry. He believes stories and poetry should be the root of initiating everlasting change. Gary has two forthcoming books: *How to survive a Sheartk Attack*, after suffering a heart attack and depression, and *Go from the B of the BANG!*, a collection of his struggles in dealing with race.

Dane Ince traveled from his Texas place of birth to Berkeley, California, to study art. He resides sheltering in place in San Francisco. William S. Burroughs and South American writer Jorge Luis Borges are some of his favorites. He is on the Beat-dada spectrum between Marcel Duchamp and Andrew Goldsworthy.

Poet and artist **Henry L. Jones** delves deeply with words and art. The Fisk University alum's book is *Run into Blackness*. Featured Poet in: *Chapter 16*, *Black Voices Matter*, *Poet's Corner*, and *Poets Vote*. Over 30 publications published his poems. Some recent awards: Art Wire Fellow and City Poet Laureate.

Allison Boyd Justus is a teacher, consultant, and the author of *Solstice to Solstice to Solstice: A Year of Sunrises in Poetry* (Alternating Current Press, 2017). She earned her MFA in Creative Writing and Environment from Iowa State University in 2021. Find her at www.allisonboydjustus. com.

The poet **K H A O S** is a mixture of old school griot and modern day storyteller. He is an oral historian, writer, actor, teacher, mentor, and political activist in Nashville, Tennessee. K H A O S attended TSU and is a board member of Gideon's Army for the Defense of Children.

As an artist, **Kana Kavon** explores ancestral connections, the layers of sensuous love, and the transcendent capacities of the human spirit. Her chapbooks include *Born in Brazil* (2011) and *The Skin and Seed of Love* (2021). Kana is also an author of educational curricula and books for children and teens.

Franchesa Kirkpatrick is a Nashville, TN-native world traveler. She has been a writer and storyteller from a young age. Franchesa has had poems published in the Library of Poetry, Vanderbilt Ingram Cancer Center Anthologies and online magazines such as *Medium* and *Views Hound*. She reads at Poetry in the Brew, Literature Cafe Global and in Poetry Zooms around the world. Instagram @Franchesapic, www.youtube.com/Franchesavideos

P W Lea lives in Nashville with his dog the Bad Boy.

Ananda Lima is the author of the poetry collection *Mother/land* (Black Lawrence Press, 2021), and three chapbooks: *Translation* (Paper Nautilus, 2019), *Amblyopia* (Bull City Press, 2020), and *Tropicália* (Newfound, 2021). Her work has appeared in *The American Poetry Review*, *Poets.org*, *Kenyon Review Online*, *Gulf Coast*, and elsewhere.

Carl Lowe was born in New York City and has authored more than 15 non-fiction books. He's played fiddle behind chicken wire in Texas, sung remarkably off-key on national TV, spent a year as the food editor of *Self Magazine* and has been gluten-free since 2006 (thank you, celiac!).

Dana Malone's a Nashville-based poet and storyteller, who's featured at the Brew and was part of its previous iterations, going back to 1991. Since 03.26.2020, she's performed daily for Nashville and the community at-large through Music City Sings at 6 (Follow #musiccitysingsat6, @ dana_malone_writer on socials).

Nashville's very own ever so loved and familiar face in the spoken word scene is: **MAMA**. MAMA. incorporates her technical study of theatre and language arts into a beautiful medley of pain, passion, precision, and presence when she presents to the people. When asked what her influences are, she simply responds, "life, and all that's in her." MAMA. is an inner•g felt by those she reflects. She looks like truth, from all perspectives. Purpose: to heal.

Des Mannay is a Welsh writer of colour. First poetry collection, *Sod 'em – and tomorrow* published by Waterloo Press. Co-editor *The Angry Manifesto journal*. Claimed top honours in 4 poetry competitions and shortlisted in 7 others. Performed at numerous venues/festivals, and published in various poetry journals. Work in 24 poetry anthologies.

Noel Marie is an artist, writer, certified yoga teacher, and advocate based in Nashville. Originally from New Jersey, Noel Marie graduated from La Salle University with a dual bachelor's degree in public relations and communication management. A lot of her writing derives from exploring the darkness and light in her experiences and dreams.

Kat Marsh is an author, poet, speaker, and calligrapher from Tennessee. She has contributed to film projects, anthologies, and celebrations that shine her calling. Her first book, *InkWielder: Case Study from a Paper Couch*, was published in 2021. To learn more, connect at www.lrdrkat.com.

Caroline Minter is a native of Chicago, Illinois, who enjoys doing workshops with the Chicago Poetry Foundation, creatively crafting her gift for others through various outlets, loves sharing during open mics and has been a feature on several scenes. Her first book of poetry entitled, *Words of My Mouth*, is scheduled for release this year.

A Pushcart Prize and Best of the Net-nominee, **Elaine Nadal** is the author of two poetry books: *When* and *Sweat, Dance, Sing, Cut*, published by Finishing Line Press. Her work has appeared in several journals, including *Beyond Words Literary Magazine*, *Haunted Waters Press*, *Hoot Review*, and *Latino Book Review Magazine*.

Zach Nicholson: "I'm a writer and musician turned software developer, but I still find the time to write a poem or play the piano when I'm moody. I also participate every year in NaNoWriMo, and you should, too!"

Reese North was born in Newcastle NSW Australia. He began writing poetry as a child and developed his unique voice through his adult years. In 1995, he performed his poetry at the Sydney Opera House, and his work was visually represented in 2003. He continues to evolve his style.

Joshua Edward Parrish grew up on the Harpeth river outside of Nashville. He is a communist with a passion for reading, writing, and the natural world. He is now a Nationally Registered EMT living and working in Missoula, Montana with his girlfriend.

Phynne~Belle (Tricia De Jesus-Gutierrez) is a poet, blogger, and podcaster. She hosts a podcast, as well as an open mic weekly, both named Phynnecabulary. She has one poetry collection published in 2017, titled *Some Days, Here*, and resides in the SF Bay Area amidst the chaos of too many pets.

Shawn Renee is a Tennessee native and a fledgling in the poetry community, but words pour from her like water, and it delights her to no end when they nourish and feed the soul of another. Don't try and find her. She'll find you.

JR Robles has a long history of questionable decisions, but one of the best he ever made was to check out an open mic one night at Poetry in the Brew. He's a writer, actor, filmmaker, and teacher who lives in Nashville, TN.

Born **Sergio Ramon Rodriguez**, nicknamed "Serge," I gave myself the androgynous pen name, "Sir-Reyna Lucio." The Murder Capital of the World, a destructive-doomsday cult, and my severely-profoundly disabled sister shaped my stories of race, class, and ability. We will die giving these stories to those who need them most.

Tricia Schwaab has written since childhood, filling notebooks with stories and poems. Her poetry has been published in journals including *Calliope*, *Dead Snakes*, and *20/20 Vision: Focus on Czech Republic*. She has also had plays produced, including her first full-length play, *When The Letter Writers Have All Died.*

Landrew Sevel: "My poems are about their process. I also practice as a psychologist and study pain, the body, and trauma. I find solace in movement."

Denver resident **Michael Sindler's** compositions span numerous genres. He's appeared in various regional and national print and web publications, including *2020: The Year America Changed* anthology. He's collaborated in numerous media bridging projects and performances.

Meg Smith is writer, journalist, dancer, and events producer living in Lowell, Mass. Her poetry and fiction have recently appeared in *Muddy River Poetry Review*, *The Cafe Review*, *Poetry Bay*, *Polarity*, *Raven Cage*, *Sirens Call*, and many more. She is the author of five poetry books and a short fiction collection, *The Plague Confessor*. She welcomes visits to megsmithwriter.com, Facebook.com/megsmithwriter, and Twitter @MegSmith_Writer.

Regan Smith is an author and poet based in Pataskala, Ohio. She pens poetry with a purpose: to evoke healing, reflection, and growth. When she's not writing, she's sipping herbal tea, propagating plants, and ventures out into forests.

Kimberly Jay aka Special K's in a long term and mostly committed relationship with words. She uses them to play with imaginations, tantalize thoughts, or provoke out of the box thinking. Tastier than any cereal and more habit forming than any drug—Special K dares you to get addicted to her spoken words.

Dennis Stefanov: "I use letters to form words to form sentences to form something else entirely."

Markey Mark Symmonds is a written and spoken word poet from Northamptonshire, UK, who performs at open mic nights worldwide. His freestyle poetry has been published in five anthologies and online journals. Mark has just released his first poetry collection, *Rhythm of the Ink—The First Wave.*

Andi Talbot (he/they) is a Pushcart nominated poet and photographer from Newcastle, England. They have released two chapbooks, *Burn Before Reading* (2019) and *Old Wounds//New Skin* (2020), both via Analog Submission Press. They are also the co-host of the CPCL open mic event and poetry editor for *Periwinkle Lit Mag.*

Edith Tapia "Blackbird" is a queer writer/poet/performer with a "Declamation Style" from Mexico. There, she won second place in a statewide and in a nationwide poetry contest. Sonora University published her in 2017. Now in the USA, she was featured in Malvern Books and in the Waterfront Festival.

Anti-racism, gender, protests, love, abuse, mental health, cats—all subjects in **Rhoda Thomas'** five poetry collections, drawn from university teaching, therapy, personal loss, and activism. Co-founder of Live Poets Society in Wales UK, she regularly hosts and contributes to poetry events.

After 20+ years in the healthcare industry, **Katie Thompson** is currently a stay-at-home mom to a beautiful 9-year-old daughter. She is finally fulfilling her dreams of becoming a writer, artist, and designer, as well as returning to college part-time. She has been published in Vanderbilt-Ingram Cancer Center's *Momentum* and *Where I'm From*.

Jon Wesick is a regional editor of the *San Diego Poetry Annual*. He's published hundreds of poems and stories in journals such as the *Atlanta Review, Berkeley Fiction Review, Metal Scratches, Pearl, Slipstream, Space and Time, Tales of the Talisman,* and *Zahir*. Jon is the author of the poetry collections *Words of Power, Dances of Freedom,* and *A Foreigner Wherever I Go* as well as several novels and short story collections. His most recent novel is *The Enigma Brokers*. http://jonwesick.com

Born and raised in the heart of Nashville, **Gabby White** explores the different valleys that are poetry. Where she was once left trying to navigate a lost sense of direction within her spirit, along came poetry to nourish her. In her down time, you can usually catch her blowing kisses out a window, lying around in a field with another's work of art, or bouncing around the Earth with pure, unfiltered bliss.

Donna Krupkin Whitney is a retired neurologist and a member of the pastoral staff of Metropolitan Interdenominational Church in Nashville. She thanks her friends K.H.A.O.S and Sizwe for helping her discover her poetic voice.

Skylar J Wynter, best-selling author of a poetry and flash fiction collection entitled *Pieces of Humanity*, resides in Perth, Western Australia. When not writing, Wynter can be found in the virtual arena of online poetry events such as Poetry in the Brew. Her second book of poetry and art will be released in October 2021.

Ray Zimmerman is a poet and a freelance journalist living in Chattanooga, Tennessee. His poems have appeared *The Southern Poetry Review: Tennessee* from Texas Review Press and in other fine publications. He grew up near Canton, Ohio, within a short distance of an oil refinery and an abandoned strip mine.

Recent Titles from April Gloaming

Dear Excavator by Evan D. Williams

Black Lives Rising by Chiatulah Ameke

The World Black, Beautiful, and Beast by C.I. Aki

The Superior Act of Presenting Your Teeth to Strangers by MD Marcus

Even in the Quiet Places by Christopher K. Doyle

Old Field Pines by C.F. Lindsey

9 781953 932068